CW01305452

RECOVERING THE SELF

Essays on Babaji's Kriya Yoga

Nacho Albalat, Nityananda

Copyright © 2013 Nacho Albalat, Nityananda

Edited by Durga Ahlund and Govindan Satchidananda. Thank you both so much for your work!

ISBN: 9798645590628
Imprint: Independently published

All rights reserved. No part of this book may be reproduced or utilized in any form or by any means, electronic or mechanical, including photocopying, recording, or by any information storage and retrieval system, without permission in writing from the publisher.

Contents

Introduction	9
Essays on Babaji's Kriya Yoga	11
The only treasure	11
Babaji's Kriya Yoga, a lineage of Yoga	13
Tantra, the weave of consciousness	17
Building the perfect temple of bliss	21
An electric circuit for a higher consciousness	26
The bliss of now	29
Meditation is liberation	31
Yoga versus habitual patterns of conduct	36
Mataji and her nightly meditation	39
Mantras: tuning to higher frequencies	43
The power of the Name	45
The Tantra of the 18 Siddhas	50
Recovering the Self	57
The Yoga of emotions	61
Emotional basis for peace	65
The ego and the dance of Shiva	72
Integrated experiences – dissociated experiences	75
The heat of Kundalini	78
The poison that Shiva drank	81
The commotion of samadhi	85
Bhakti Yoga: the bliss of love	89
Appendix: Beginning Babaji's Kriya Yoga	93
Glossary	95
Bibliography	97

RECOVERING THE SELF

Essays on Babaji's Kriya Yoga

Introduction

The objective of this book is twofold:

- To offer an introduction to Kriya Yoga to all those who are thinking to be initiated in its techniques.

- To support you in the practice of Babaji's Kriya Yoga, by offering clear explanations of its objectives and effects.

After years of practice, it is a pleasure for me to share my understanding about this path, with the sole intention that others could benefit from it. It expresses my gratitude for all that I received from those who preceded me.

I must point out that my understanding of these teachings – and my fascination with them – changes as I practice and teach them; I have been writing these texts – and rewriting them – for many years. I'm sure that all devoted students of Kriya Yoga have interesting things to tell... my wish is that you will be one of them.

Affectionately.

Con cariño,

Nacho Albalat, Nityananda

info@ kriyayogadebabaji.net
www.kriyayogadebabaji.net

Essays on Babaji's Kriya Yoga

The only treasure

When you are sleeping and dreaming you create universes, with experiences that makes you happy or makes you suffer. When you awake from the dream, you may think "how foolish was what I felt in the dream" – you understand that everything was a creation of your mind. But until you awake from the dream, until you change your state of consciousness from the dream state to the physical sense state, you are not able to understand this. In the dream state, what you lived, sad or happy, was real.

Similarly, our physical reality is also a creation of the mind, and it is necessary to awake to another state of consciousness, higher than the physical sense state, to realize this. Some would label this higher state "cosmic consciousness," although it can have many names.

A "satguru" is someone who has awakened to this state of consciousness, and, under certain conditions, can transmit this state to others, the same as a candle flame can light another candle.

Different religions have been founded by human beings who experienced this cosmic consciousness, and they described it with different images, according to their experiences. These images range from the more personal ones (like the images of Jesus) to the more impersonal ones (like the images of Buddha). These different founders also transmitted their higher state of consciousness to their closest followers.

However, as is often the case, those that became the political leaders of these religions did not acquire the state of consciousness of the founders. Religious leaders substituted rites and the worship of metaphorical images for the experience of higher consciousness that was originally transmitted by their founders.

A satguru doesn't offer creeds or religious ideologies, but the real experience of cosmic consciousness. In the physical presence of a satguru one can experience an ineffable peace and bliss that no ideology can grant.

The difficulty lies then, in finding a true satguru; there is no a higher treasure in the universe. His or her grace is the door to cosmic consciousness.

Finding the Satguru

It is said that you don't choose a master, but you are chosen by the master. It is also said that when the disciple is ready, the master appears.

So the best way to find a satguru is to prepare oneself for it. The masters prescribe a yogic discipline or "sadhana" that the disciple must follow. The closer the relationship between them, the more personalized is this sadhana.

Many Yoga masters have laid down sadhanas that anyone can follow, according their orientation and preferences. The different lineages of Yoga offer immense riches of teachings and techniques that one can follow. The goal of all these teachings and techniques is to find everlasting bliss and happiness; this is what all human beings are looking for, in some way or another.

By following one of these sadhanas, the student can also receive the grace of the master or masters of that lineage. And sometimes, after this effort, the student can find a living realized master.

So the way to receive the blessings of a satguru, in some way or another, is to follow a sadhana laid down by a master.

Babaji's Kriya Yoga, a lineage of Yoga

Babaji's Kriya Yoga is a lineage or an authentic path of Yoga, one of many, which comes, as the name indicates, from a great master of Yoga known as "Babaji."

Babaji became first known in the West through the book, "Autobiography of a Yogi," written by Paramahansa Yogananda, published in the United States in 1946. The chapter XXXIII of this book describes an immortal master that resides in the valley of Badrinath, Himalayas, who always retains the appearance of a young man.

Babaji as appears in the book "Autobiography of a Yogi"

Yogananda relates how in 1861 Babaji taught Lahiri Mahasya a series of yogic techniques near the town of Ranikhet, in the Himalayas. Afterwards, during the rest of his life, Lahiri Mahasaya taught these techniques in the holy north India city of

Benares to many disciples; this Yoga would be known as "Kriya Yoga". Yogananda received these techniques from his master, Sri Yukteshwar, a disciple of Lahiri, and after travelling to the United States, spread them through his organization "Self-Realization Fellowship". His book, "Autobiography of a Yogi," has been translated into thirty-five languages, introducing Babaji and Kriya Yoga world-wide.

In 1952, after the death of Yogananda, Babaji brought together and communicated with with two men of South India, V.T. Neelakantan and S.A.A. Ramaiah. Over a period of several years, V.T. Neelakantan was granted nightly visits by Babaji, resulting in the publication of three books. Babaji dictated to and inspired V.T. Neelakantan to write about Kriya Yoga and the important role of spirituality in the life of man. These three books have been republished in one volume called, "The Voice of Babaji" (Kriya Yoga and Publications 2003).

For his part, S.A.A. Ramaiah was with Babaji in Badrinath in 1954, and received from him 144 kriyas or techniques of Kriya Yoga. Since then, until his passing in 2006, Yogi Ramaiah – Yogiar – taught theses techniques throughout the world, serving Babaji in different projects, including the construction of temples and centers of Kriya Yoga.

This Kriya Yoga crystallizes the monistic theistic Siddhanta philosophy of the Siddhas, the perfected masters of South of India. Yogananda presented Kriya Yoga in the context of Vedanta philosophy, as expressed in the Bhagavad Gita.

Vedanta emphasizes the transcendence of this illusionary world reality with the goal of attaining "moksha," liberation from the cycle of reincarnation.

Siddhanta emphasizes the transformation, not the transcendence, of our human nature, so the Divine can fully manifest in the world. As such it is part of the tantric tradition. The teachings of Lahiri Mahasaya were also from the tantric tradition.

Marshall Govindan Satchidananda, a disciple of Babaji and long time student of Yoga Ramaiah, founded the Babaji's Kriya Yoga Order of Acharyas, with the goal of creating a core of skilled and dedicated teachers for dissemination of these 144 kriyas or yogic techniques world-wide.

Different lineages of Kriya Yoga

There are different lineages of Kriya Yoga:

- The teachers of all or some of the 144 yogic techniques that Yogi Ramaiah received from Babaji in 1954.

Yogi Ramaiah    Govindan Satchidananda

- The teachers of all or some of the techniques that Lahiri Mahasaya received from Babaji in 1861. The numerous disciples of Lahiri Mahasay taught, in turn, some of these techniques to others, including some variations.

- The techniques which Babaji taught to Swami Sivananda in Rishikesh, which he in turn taught to his disciple Swami Satyananda Saraswati, who taught and even published some of them in books.

Why do these different lineages exist? Babaji gives different techniques to different people according to their needs and the context of their time. An individual, according to his own temperament and potential is given particular techniques and teachings. If practiced with discipline and dedication, these will bring particular personal benefits, spiritual and worldly. At least, this is our view from the standpoint of Babaji's Kriya Yoga.

Although each of the various lineages teaches different techniques, their commonality lies in their source, Babaji, and in the primary importance given to spinal breathing. Kriya pranayamas move energy within subtle channels in the spinal column. The aim is to activate "kundalini," the potential power and consciousness, which will accelerate the student's spiritual evolution. This approach is Tantric, the Yoga of transformation, the most recent form of Yoga.

Tantra, the weave of consciousness

Tantra developed as Yoga evolved. One can point to its' beginnings in the fifth century, A.D. The evolution of Tantra Yoga took hundreds of years during the Kali Yuga, the present Dark Age, when the Siddhas, the perfected masters of Yoga, recognized the need to overcome the huge obstacles to concentration and meditation.

The spiritual practices and teachings of Classical Yoga and Vedanta were becoming less and less effective. The mind of most people was too restless and agitated. Tantric practices included the awakening of kundalini and the psycho-physical centers, or chakras, as a result of great experimentation by the Siddhas.

Classical Yoga, as recorded by Patanjali in his *Yoga Sutras* (second century B.C.), seeks the pure principle of consciousness, separated from Nature and its manifestations. The yogi focuses on that which lies behind the reality of the impermanent phenomenal world. In this fundamental text of Yoga by Patanjali there isn't any mention of kundalini, *chakras* or how to activate them, nor the manipulation of the energy or *Shakti*. What is emphasized is the progressive development of mental concentration, leading to absorption in pure consciousness, known as s*amadhi,* untied from the phenomena of Nature.

Classical Yoga proposes asceticism, including withdrawal from the world of the physical senses, the main sources of distraction for yogis. This path is useful if you retire to the desert, to a monastery or a cave of the Himalayas, removing as much as possible any source of sensorial distraction. The alternative approach to asceticism, Tantra, developed by the Siddhas, instead of withdrawing from the physical senses, includes them in the spiritual practices. Instead of ignoring energy, let us use it! Everything can be useful in Tantra; everything is used and included in the spiritual practice. In fact, the word "Tantra" means "weave" or "net". Everything is interwoven and entwined! Why separate between "divine" and "not divine," if the Divine is equally present in everything?

Therefore, Tantra, as spiritual path, is very useful if one doesn't retire from the world – everybody can follow it, even householders. Tantra is an approach that values the dynamic or feminine aspect of the Divine: the energy that gives form to everything (*Shakti*), and not only its static or masculine aspect, consciousness (*Shiva*) – emphasized in Classical Yoga.

Concentrating energies

The tantric method pursues the same goal of Classical Yoga, reaching the pure non-dual consciousness, anchored in the bliss and peace of the Self, which is not lost in the distraction of the impermanent phenomena. And our best ally for this is the same divine Energy that creates these phenomena. The Siddhas say: "the same thing that makes us stumble can help us to get up". So, the tantric approach is quite energetic. There appears then the *Kundalini Yoga*, which works with the essential energy hiding in each human being. This energy is capable of leading one to higher states of consciousness.

The book *Hatha Yoga Pradipika*, written in the XV century A.D., openly offers *asanas*, *pranayamas*, techniques to activate the *chakras* and Kundalini energy. In this approach, instead of using the mind, let us work with the vital energy responsible of the functioning of the body and the mind. By doing so, in an indirect way, we can work on the mind and its states of consciousness, something that we can't do from a mere mental concentration.

The Yoga Siddhas discovered that we have seven subtle centers of consciousness along the spine, each one associated with a different psychological state. . They also discovered that if we can concentrate our vital energy in the higher centers, in the top of the head, we can experience higher states of consciousness. And the yogis thought: What is the most powerful manifestation of human vital energy…? You guessed it!

Yes, sex is such energy. Tantric Yoga or Kundalini Yoga sublimates our sexual energy up into the higher centers of consciousness in order to activate them. This is energetic transmutation, "alchemy," transmuting the lead of passions into the gold of spirituality. Many true spiritual traditions, like Taoism in China work with this energy. Even in Mexico there is Quetzalcoatl, the feathered serpent.

Therefore, the goal of the different tools that Tantra offers (*asanas*, *pranayamas*, muscular locks, *mantras*, etc.) is the sublimation of vital energy into spiritual energy and the opening of the higher centers of awareness. With that, we open the door of Heaven and experience the higher states of consciousness, looking for the irrevocable union with the Absolute, pure or cosmic consciousness – coming home.

Much more than sex

In the West, as "Yoga" has been reduced to the practice of asanas, now the word "Tantra" is understood as a yogic sexual practice. Many workshops on so-called "Tantra" are offered, in search of a super-orgasm, without conceptual or emotional limitations. But Tantra includes everything! Work, meals, relationships… it is the weave of life, with or without sex. In fact, of the 144 kriyas or techniques of Babaji's Kriya Yoga only a few of them have to do with sex. All of them have to do with the development of consciousness.

The path of Tantra develops in us a steady higher consciousness; installing the Self in the midst of daily phenomena, totally present in them, yet not swept away by them.

The Siddhas consider the sexual act to be sacred, whether it is done with the intention to bring an elevated soul into the world or to transmute sexual energy into sublime spiritual energy – it is always a gift between the lover and the beloved. This requires both partners in the sexual act to maintain the witness consciousness, and for the man to avoid ejaculation of his sexual fluids. A yogi uses sex as tool for transformation; he is not used by it!

This is certainly a challenge, part of challenge to maintain the perspective of the witness in all situations. But only by remaining as the witness do we have the chance to experience peace and bliss. It is so much easier to identify with, and be swept along by, the whirlwinds of life. We are all called to play "the game of consciousness" – Babaji's Kriya Yoga teaches us how to play the game and win bliss in every moment.

The Siddha Tirumular defines the realized yogi, the Siddha, as a person that can arrest breath, thought and semen at will (arresting the breath at will means to be able to enter in the state of mental silence or samadhi – the mark of a yogi with realization).

The image of Kali, dancing with frenzy over Shiva, illustrates this point.

This image shows the tantric posture, not only in sex, but in life also: the realized yogi becomes the Seer, a witness of the dance of creation, the Seen, the dance of Divine Energy, seeing equally the divine manifestation in everything that surrounds him – the weave of life – without being swept away by this changing whirlwind of phenomena. This is the true Tantra!

Building the perfect temple of bliss

One of the most impressive temples in Tamil Nadu, in South India, is the Brihadeeswarar Temple, in Tanjore. The main tower, 216 feet high, is crowned with a black stone of 81 tons and is considered the crown jewel of Tamil architecture, as the mystery remains how the stone was raised to this seemingly impossible height. All that is recounted is that the Siddha Karuvurar instructed King Rajaraja Chola in the construction of the temple. Rajaraja Chola was so pleased with the results that he ordered a shrine to Karuvurar to be built on the Temple grounds.

This temple is a good metaphor of our work in Babaji's Kriya Yoga. Our constant practice allows us to experience higher levels of bliss, as we come closer and closer to the Self. This culminates in the experience of "samadhi," the yogic trance where one is totally merged with pure consciousness, the Self or Truth, without confusion. The state of samadhi is characterized by mental silence, where we live our true nature: "Then, the Seer abides in his own true form" (*Yoga Sutras* I. 3). The state of samadhi is associated with the opening of the seventh chakra, the crown chakra. But if we want to keep the state of samadhi – the same as the big stone on the top of the tower of Brihadeeswarar temple – it is necessary to establish a firm foundation, a solid base to support it. We attain that through a firm and unwavering disciplined practice of Yoga.

Five sheaths, five disciplines

According to Yoga, our essence, the Self or the Divine, is covered by five sheaths ("koshas"), like layers of an onion, which correspond with several planes of manifestation. Each one of them is more subtle than the previous one. The first three layers are part of our daily experience:

- Physical sheath – our physical body.

- Vital sheath – the seat of our emotions and vitality.

- Mental sheath – the seat of the sense perceptions and the thoughts related to them.

- Intellectual sheath – the seat of abstract thought and discernment.

- Bliss or causal sheath – the seat of unconditional love and bliss.

The Divine, the Self, is hidden inside these sheaths, hidden inside us ("*For indeed, the kingdom of God is within you,*" Luke 17.21). How can we define this Divine? As Being-Consciousness-Bliss, without end and without limit.

The problems arising in our human condition is because the consciousness of the Self is enmeshed and identified with the five sheaths, just like sea-water held inside a bottle, tossed in the sea, is identified with the bottle containing it.

The ego is the habitual identification with the physical, vital, mental, intellectual and causal sheaths, with their particular traits and tendencies, different in each person. The ego is a contraction of the universal consciousness around phenomenal objects, including thoughts, emotions and those experienced through the five senses. The more we emphasize the "I," the more we reaffirm this contraction. The result of this is suffering, constantly experiencing the physical, emotional and mental ups and downs of life. The ego, fixated on impermanent phenomena, never finds the permanent peace and bliss it seeks.

Yoga is the process of liberating this ego-bound state of consciousness, identified with the sheaths, in order to realize Absolute Being-Consciousness-Bliss, *sat chit ananda*.

The five sheaths can be viewed as the walls of a prison, which limits the realization of our true Self. So these sheaths must be detached from, ignored or transcended if one is to move beyond them and merge with the Self. This is the approach of the Classical Yoga.

From the point of view of the tantric Siddhas of the South of India (the "18 Siddhas Tradition"), the five sheaths can become instruments for the manifestation of the Divine, our higher Self, in the creation.

The yogic practices of the Siddhas purify and perfect the sheaths, liberating the consciousness from their bonds, including ignorance, egoism, illusion and karma. Then the Self that we are can act without impediments through them, manifesting more and more its own perfection.

Babaji's Kriya Yoga has five limbs, five types of practices to perfect and integrate the five sheaths:

- Kriya Hatha Yoga – postures (asanas) and muscular locks (bandahs) for the physical sheath.

- Kriya Kundalini Pranayama – breathing techniques (pranayama) for the vital sheath.

- Kriya Dhyana Yoga – meditations for the mental sheath.
- Kriya Mantra Yoga – subtle sounds (mantras) for the intellectual sheath.

- Kriya Bhakti Yoga – devotional activities and service for the causal sheath.

"Kriya" means "action with awareness." The goal of Kriya Yoga is to bring "awareness," into all our actions, all of the planes of existence.

The word "Siddha" comes from the Tamil "citta." Citta is consciousness in its state of identification with the sheaths. A Siddha is a master of citta, a master of consciousness who has definitely removed the identification with the five sheaths, and has perfected them so they can manifest the Truth of the Self: *"Therefore you shall be perfect, just as your Father in heaven is perfect"* (Matthew 5.48).

A guided practice

The satguru is the hand that leads the aspirant out of the tangled forest of his own ego. He can guide insofar as he is beyond the forest of the egos, established in the Being-Consciousness-Bliss. Without him, the aspirant is trapped time and time again by the recurrent tendencies of his own sheaths.

The satguru prescribes a sadhana or spiritual discipline. One receives the grace of the satguru as long as one follows this prescribed spiritual discipline.

In all of the lineages of Kriya Yoga there is only one satguru, Babaji; the student learns to develop a direct and personal relationship with him, without intermediaries, through the seventh meditation technique, taught in the first initiation. However, the student can use this same technique to contact any spiritual master… and Babaji won't be jealous. We can deduce from this that Kriya Yoga is not a cult of personality around the person of Babaji; anyone can practice it, no matter their belief, philosophy, or condition. It is not a required to believe in anything to practice it; the student is just encouraged to practice the different techniques and to experience by himself the results.

An electric circuit for a higher consciousness

Our vital body is an energetic body, formed by "prana" (vital energy), which animates the physical body. We could compare it with an electric circuit, with its wires that transmits electricity, its resistors and transistors. The energy channels of the vital, the "nadis," would be the electric wires; the resistors would be the blocks we have in the nadis, blocks with a mental or emotional origin, and which restrict the movement of energy, with consequent heat, discomfort and disturbances. The transistors would be the psycho-energetic centers, the "chakras," each of them able to produce different functions and activities, when they are fully activated. If they are not activated, electricity just can't pass through them. They remain zones of darkness, and their potential gifts are then hidden.

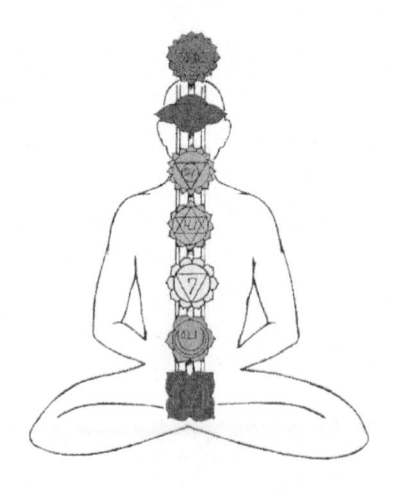

The chakras could be, in the words of Jesus, talents or analogously, coins, which are given to us, so we could make use of them at some time in our life. We can work with them or just ignore them and bury them below the soil. In this last case – following the Parable of the Talents of Jesus (Matthew 25.14-30) – our life doesn't bear fruit, and the owner of the talents, our Higher Being, finally demands them back, considering that out present incarnation is useless. However, to those who cultivate the chakras, it is said: *"Enter into the bliss of your Lord."*

Activating the circuit

Yoga explains that each chakra is related to a psychological state of consciousness, and that our actual psychological state of consciousness is a reflection to which vital energy has accumulated in a particular chakra. Greater the accumulation of vital energy in a chakra, greater the realization of the chakra's corresponding psychological potential.

Yogi Ramaiah says that our vital energetic system could bear, so to say, a power of 10 volts, and Babaji has a power of 10.000 volts. So, by raising our power to the same level of Babaji, we will be able to contact him. And, by raising our power to the same power of God, we will be able to experience God. Yogi Ramaiah remarks that through the regular practice of pranayama (breathing yogic exercises) we can increase daily the power of our vital circuitry.

"Samadhi" or yogic trance, the state of consciousness corresponding to the crown chakra, is being in pure consciousness, our true nature, according to the Siddhas (*Yoga Sutras*, I.3). This demands a very high level of energy. Therefore, the vital body, and our nervous system which supports it, must be prepared.

For this reason the work with the energy in our physical and vital bodies allows us to experience higher states of consciousness; this work is the foundation that holds the experience of samadhi, the opening of the seventh chakra on the top of the head, and our spiritual growth in consciousness.

A consistent practice of Kriya Yoga, especially the pranayama called "Kriya Kundalini Pranayama," will bring a smooth and regular increase of prana, energy, throughout all of the chakras. We build the experience of samadhi, brick by brick, integrating each aspect of our lives, without leaving anything outside.

The foundations of the practice

To create a temple worthy of divine consciousness we must do the work required to cleanse the nadis and activate the chakras.

The practice of yogic postures or asanas begins this process. Along with the first meditation technique, they constitute the foundation of our temple. It is very important to cleanse and purify the physical body and the subconscious of constricting and painful physical-emotional blocks, which impedes the free flow of energy and creates restlessness and agitation in the consciousness moving through it.

The chakras play an essential role in the experience of samadhi. Each of them are like a transistor in an electric circuit, which must be activated for a full performance of the system. The more activated the chakras are, the higher levels of energy are supported by the circuit, and therefore, one can experience higher and mores expanded levels of consciousness.

The practice of Kundalini Pranayama activates the energy from the first chakra and distributes it through all the chakras, concentrating it in the crown of the head. Later, in the second initiation, the students can receive the seed sounds or mantras to activate the chakras opening. The repetition of mantras activates and purifies the energetic system. And in the third initiation the students receive a series of kriyas that combine meditations, mantras and asanas for a more specific work over these psychic-energetic centers.

All this work we do building our inner temple is done in a gradual and integrated way, without the disturbances that require us to renounce the world; on the contrary, we in fact, embrace the world in our experience of growth. Babaji's Kriya Yoga is a jewel in the Tantric tradition, which integrates spirituality with daily life; a Yoga quite simple to follow, not spectacular, but profoundly effective at all levels of our human nature.

The bliss of now

Yoga teaches that we are neither our body nor our mind. We constantly experience our body, our mind and our emotions, but we are not these. The yogi doesn't try, nevertheless, to ignore or to repress these experiences, but rather seeks to remain very conscious of them. How? By keeping the attitude of the witness, observing everything that happens in his consciousness, watching the drama – or the comedy – of life that is happening around and inside him.

By keeping the watchful attitude of the witness the yogi is not carried away by the play of life. For example, one can think "it is sad that today is cloudy," and, in that moment, by one's identification with that thought, the body gets depressed, or sad, and various parts of the physical organism respond consequently. We all do this, more or less; we are carried away by the first thought that crosses our mind, no matter what. It is like being as foolish as to walk in the street and to eat the first thing you find on the sidewalk.

The yogi, on the other hand, keeps a watchful and conscious attitude, and as the thought "it is sad that today is cloudy" appears, he can think next: "this is only a thought, I can accept it or not, or I can choose to think that now I am in peace," or he can also think: "a ridiculous thought has entered in my head."

The more one develops the attitude of the witness regarding everything, the more blissful becomes his or her life. Because the attitude of being aware, being conscious, brings bliss. Usually we associate happiness with a certain external event, but all the external events are temporary, they come and go. Bliss is a gentle and constant joy, unconditional and so doesn't depend on anything. Yoga teaches us that bliss is the state of our soul, our true Self. And the less we identify ourselves with what we are not (the body, the mind, the emotions) through the voluntary development of our witness consciousness, the more we experience our bliss, our true Self.

So, the bliss we are all looking for, we already have, here and now. But few of us live in the now, although this is the only real place, the only place where we can exist. The mind, the thief of awareness, loves to live in the past or in the future: what I did, what the other did to me, what I will have in the future to be happy, the future material or spiritual experience that I must attain… etc. The truth is that neither the past or future exist, both are only daydreams of the mind. The Siddhas said that "we are dreaming with our eyes open." We only have the now.

The more one witnesses his mind at work; the less power it has over you. The mind is an instrument, the same as the body, and must be used, but one should not be used by it. Babaji's Kriya Yoga offers several techniques to learn to master the mind and develop the consciousness or the state of the witness. This is attained through the yogic discipline. As one develops constantly this state, there is a moment when life becomes more and more interesting and blissful, no matter what happens.

Meditation is liberation

The ultimate reality is pure consciousness, where we cease to identify with stuff, through the instrument of our mind. *"The mind acts as a medium of communication between spirit and matter. It is just a ladder making a man climb up to the realm of Supreme Bliss or making him climb down to the deep abyss of ignorance"* says the book "The Voice of Babaji."[1] So, in our meditations we take charge of the creator of our reality: our own mind.

What is left when we remove the thoughts from our mind? The same as when a cinema movie is over, what is left a white light screen. The same as when a movie at the cinema is over, there is only a white light screen. The same thing happens with our mind in the morning, just when we are awakening, before we make the slightest physical or mental movement. For a few moments each morning we experience a purely blissful, luminous mental screen, before the mind has a chance to remind us who and where we are. The Yoga Vasishtha says: *"Consciousness is the only essential reality, in sleep as in waking. It is the Lord, the supreme truth: you are That, I am That, and everything that is, is That."*[2]

The Siddhas called this pure space of light "Vettaveli" or vast luminous space of liberation. They entered more and more into this luminous space of pure consciousness. *"When the movement of the mind has ceased, the self shines with its own light, where suffering is dissolved and bliss reigns, which is the experience of the self in the self."*[3]

When we observe our own mind, in the different meditations, we come out of the phenomenal plane, the plane of the created world, and we come closer to the creator. Meditation is, therefore, a space of liberation, which takes us away from the conditioned and brings us closer to the creator of the conditioned. Then we become conscious of the lenses through which we observe the world, and if we observe enough with our own mind, we can change these lenses, or remove them once and for all.

The different visualizations of Babaji's Kriya Yoga allow us to become conscious of our own creator process – a process that is always active, no matter if we notice it or not. To master this process allow us, eventually, to stop it. Or we can recreate at our own convenience. *"Mind is again a master weaver. Mind weaves the inner garment of character and the outer garment of circumstances. So, what he has hitherto woven in ignorance and darkness, he may now unweave in enlightenment and brightness"* says "The Voice of Babaji."[4] The yogis with spiritual realization show an amazing mastery over the physical reality, that some would call "miraculous." This is the tantric method, which doesn't reject the world, but uses it as a tool for transformation.

The fundamental goal of meditation is becoming aware of one's own consciousness, the luminous and blissful screen (so to say) behind everything, the space between us and the creation, the space of pure being between the thoughts. As long as one meditates, one discovers more and more that this space of liberation, Vettaveli, is more and more everywhere, in every moment.

Understanding Kriya Yoga Meditations

There is sometimes a lack of understanding of what Babaji's Kriya Yoga meditations or *dhyanas* are, and their purpose and goal. Many people, when talking about Yoga meditation, think that it is about "leaving the mind blank." The right words would be to talk about "quieting the mind," although a meditation can include much more than that.

In Kriya Yoga we define the practice of meditation, Dhyana Yoga, as "the scientific art of mastering the mind." It is not a question of nullifying the mind, but of mastering it. Normally our own mind dominates us, we are physically and emotionally subject to any of its occurrences, unless we carry out the work of taking care of it.

The mind is a creative instrument that we constantly use, whether we are aware of it or not. With it we create and recreate our personal reality:

If you believe yoursel to be a creature of outside conditions then you will be bufetedby circumstances right through. Realize that you are the creative power and you can command the hidden soil and seeds of your being, out of which circumstances grow. (...)The outer world of circumstances sharpens itself according to the inner world of thoughts. Circumstances do not make you, but they reveal you.

- The Voice of Babaji[5]

Accepting that we create from our minds the circumstances that surround us, consciously or unconsciously, means abandoning victimhood and assuming our own power. So if we want to take charge of the circumstances around our life, we will have to start by taking charge of what is happening in our minds. We can also create from a full consciousness everything we create from our unconsciousness. And here comes the role of the *dhyanas* or Kriya Yoga meditations.

Recreating our circumstances

The word "Siddha", which designates the realized masters of Yoga, is related with the word "siddhi", which means "perfection", and also refers to the "yogic powers." Yoga has tools to awaken all human potential, including what some call yogic powers, which are nothing but possibilities of growth within our reach. The tools for this are the mastering of the mind and the mastering of *prana*, the vital energy.

Mastering the mind would be something as basic as being able to think what you want to think and not thinking to not what you don't want to think, in a sustained way. Something as simple as this, but is there anyone who can do it for even three minutes?

The first two of the seven meditations taught in the first initiation of Kriya Yoga help develop these two capacities. Then, with the following meditations, we learn to do more things: to visualize and recreate what we want to manifest in our lives and to develop our intellectual discernment, our intuition and our connection to superconsciousness (Babaji).

All of these skills go beyond just leaving your mind blank; they involve developing its latent possibilities, unfolding our human potential. That is the way of the Siddhas. And even if we do not reach the yogic realization that they reached, the cultivation of these meditations can help us to improve the circumstances that surround us.

The student must understand that it is essential that we bring to our daily lives the achievement obtained through the practice of meditation: the ability to detach, to visualize what we want to create, intuition and inspiration. Meditation is not an activity disassociated from the rest of our existence, but an activity designed to intertwine with it and transform it. Only then does the practice of Kriya Yoga take on its full meaning, and it also becomes a way of life.

A dynamic Yoga

This approach of the Kriya meditations is within the tantric orientation of the lineage of the Siddhas. Classical Yoga just seeks to transcend and leave behind the world, the mind and the senses, to achieve liberation; it is a Yoga for renunciates. Tantric Yoga involves the world, the mind and the senses in the spiritual experience. The word "tantra" means "network" or "weave." The Divine is woven into our ordinary life, and the Siddha appreciates the play of the Divine, even with the five senses. If the Divine is in everything, where can one flee to? What is needed is a transformation one's point of view to perceive this Divine; it takes "having eyes to see".

The tantric approach is in tune with the circumstances of this current era:

Humanity of the twentieth century is dominated by rajas (dynamism). *Activity consciously charged with high tension characterizes the daily round of the average man everywhere (...) This passion for extreme activity cannot be repressed. (...) Yoga, too, has to assume the aspect of being readily practicable to all. All activity is unavoidable; Yoga has to be attained in and through activity.*

(...) Sadhana should not imply a divorce and severance from normal life. The latter will itself become a dynamic sadhana through a shifting of your angle of vision.

- The Voice of Babaji[6]

In the third initiation of Kriya Yoga the student learns to quiet and stop the mind and the breath to enter in the state of *samadhi* or cognitive absorption, and thus experience pure consciousness, the Self. However, such stillness can already be experienced from the first initiation by practicing the first meditation technique or the Kriya Kundalini Pranayama.

The mastery of the mind that achieved by practicing the seven meditations of the first initiation helps also to quiet the mind in the later stages of sadhana. Finally the student understands and realizes that Yoga includes our whole life, encompassing both the stillness of silence and the action. Everything is equally interwoven by the Self, of which we are an inseparable part.

1- Neelakantan, V.T.N., Ramaiah, S.A.A., y Nagaraj, Babaji. (2003). *La voz de Babaji; una trilogía de Kriya Yoga*. St. Etienne de Bolton, Québec: Babaji's Kriya Yoga and Publications. p.443.
2- (1995). *Yoga Vasishtha*. Madrid: Etnos. p.353.
3- Id., p.464.
4- *The Voice of Babaji*, p.236.
5- Id., p.236.
6- Id., pp.212-213.

Yoga versus habitual patterns of conduct

The Siddhas say that Yoga is the process of cleansing the modifications that arise from the subconscious mind (*Yoga Sutras* I.2). We all have a subconscious mind where our habitual tendencies of conduct are stored. We tend to be mistrustful, or dubious, or inconstant, or tend to get angry easily, or any other thing, because of the patterns of conduct engraved in our subconscious mind. In Yoga, these patterns are called "*samskaras*" (mental impressions) or "*vasanas*" (mental tendencies).

Some say that the attachment to physical sensations is the biggest obstacle to the advancement in Yoga, but it is not the only obstacle. There is also the attachment to one's own thoughts, and the attachment to one's own negative and habitual patterns of conduct.

When one calms down the mind, one can experience the peace and the bliss of one's own Self. The different techniques of Yoga, especially the techniques of pranayama (breath control), bring mental silence. Slowly, one learns to detach from the process of thinking. One must make an effort to move the physical body. But, the mind doesn't need effort to think and it won't stop its movement through its own nature; effort is required for thoughts to cease.

As one advances in Yoga, one must face, sooner or later, his own patterns of conduct. Any honest path of growth will make its' follower aware of his or her personal limitations. In the ordinary life we don't have a chance to see our own tendencies, although we are limited by them. Usually everyone else but oneself sees them. For example, a person can have a tendency to have doubts about everything. This person applies this to everything in his life, in a conscious or unconscious way, with different results. If he practices Yoga, he will also end up doubting his practice. At the end of the day only his habit of doubting or his practice of Yoga will survive.

Usually these subconscious habits and tendencies are justified through conscious "rationalizations" or pseudo-arguments. In this way these repetitive patterns are reinforced again and again, so preventing transformation and personal growth.

In Babaji's Kriya Yoga, the first meditation technique – taught in the first initiation – is useful to cleanse and purify the subconscious mind, including one's own tendencies and samskaras. So, this technique is basic and decisive for the advancement (or progress) of the student, and is one of the foundations of yogic practice. You can stop being affected by subconscious conditioning, only if you can recognize the habitual patterns when they arise and can understand what is causing them and then consciously and consistently choose not to act under their influence.

The Bhagavad Gita narrates that Arjuna was demoralized when faced with the challenge of fighting against people he knew, some of who were his relatives. Krishna comforted him, encouraging him to battle on and fulfill his duty. This is a metaphor of the battle of yogic transformation, where, inspired by our Higher Self, Krishna, we fight against our habitual negative tendencies, our relatives.

As we advance in the practice of Kundalini Pranayama and introduce much energy in our psycho-physical system, our habitual and negative tendencies become more and more evident. In this moment we need the force given to us by the first meditation technique to let go these tendencies. Jesus refers to this truth when he says *"And no one pours new wine into old wineskins. Otherwise, the new wine will burst the skins; the wine will run out and the wineskins will be ruined"* (Luke 5.37). The great energy kundalini (the wine) generated by the practice of pranayama should not be used in the old mistaken patterns of conduct (the old wineskins), because if so, all the yogic effort is wasted. There is no advancement on the path, we merely blindly continue to follow the scripts written in our subconscious mind with even more force.

A path like Babaji's Kriya Yoga requires a personal transformation and one must do the inner cleansing. As the Kundalini energy progressively awakens, one must be able to thrive with higher levels of energy. For this reason the first meditation technique is strongly recommended, especially in the first years on the path. This practice can determinate if there is a real advancement or not.

Mataji and her nightly meditation

Mataji, the spiritual partner of Babaji, is a mysterious figure of whom we little know, apart from the references given in the books "Autobiography of a yogi" and "The Voice of Babaji."

In India is common that the saints (even the divinities) appear in a masculine form together with his feminine counterpart. The masculine aspect is like Shiva, the principle of consciousness, and the feminine aspect is Shakti, the creative power principle. As with Shiva and Shakti, the masculine principle complements the feminine principle of energy, and the feminine principle complements the masculine principle of consciousness.

It is said that Mataji has the same spiritual level of Babaji, but she has chosen the role of the disciple, serving Babaji, her master. So, she is the personification of the perfect disciple. Certainly is more difficult to find a good disciple than to find a good master. In the second initiation of Kriya Yoga the student can receive the mantra of Mataji and to develop a personal relationship with her.

A famous narrative in the "Autobiography of a Yogi" and "the Voice of Babaji" explains how Mataji made possible that Babaji retained his physical body, for the benefit of all devotees:

"Suddenly at midnight, Lahiri Mahasaya ordered the recluse, Ram Gopal Mazumdar to go alone and immediately to the

Dasasamedh ghat in Banaras. The command was carried out promptly. Ram Gopal sat at the secluded spot, and after a while was astonished to find a huge stone slab open, revealing a hidden cave, from which Mataji, the ecstatic sister of Babaji, stepped out through the yogic process of levitation. Soon after, Lahiri Mahasaya and the Kriya Paramguru materialized. All three prostrated at the feet of Babaji.

Babaji: "Propose to shed my form and plunge into the Infinite."

Mataji: "Master, (entreatingly) I have glimpsed your plan. Why should you leave your body?"

Babaji: "Because it makes no difference to be visible or invisible."

Mataji: "Gurú Deva, if it makes no difference, please do not discard your form."

¡AUM! The beloved Master consented to retain his physical body which would be visible to a selected few only. Thus, a first-rate crisis in the history of the Kriya movement was saved through the intervention of the holy sister. ¡Jai Mataji!"[1]

Mataji, the personification of compassion, made possible that Babaji could bless his devotees preserving a physical body through the ages.

Mataji in the secret ashram of Badrinath

In 1953 V.T. Neelakantan, one of the authors of "The Voice of Babaji," visited the secret ashram of Babaji in Badrinath, Himalayas, by the grace of Babaji. The book "Babaji and the 18 Siddha Kriya Yoga Tradition" records his testimony about Mataji and her work in the ashram:

"The residents included the sister (paternal cousin) of Babaji, "Mataji Nagalakshmi Deviyar" (also known as "Annai"). She was wearing a cotton sari, white in color, with a green border and a long red sash over it and around her neck. According to

him, she is a strikingly beautiful woman, with fair skin, a thin frame and is taller than her brother. Her face is rather long with high cheek bones, and resembles that of Kashi, Paramahansa Yogananda's disciple from the front, and that of Neelakantan's own wife from the side.

Annai Nagalakshmi Deviyar is in charge of organizing the ashram and serves the residents in various capacities. She supervises the preparation of a daily, simple, vegetarian meal served at noon. The meal is supportive of the yogic lifestyle of the ashram. She takes special care of a largo "tulasi" plant which sits atop a "peetam," or shrine, nearly four feet high. She daily worships "Tulasi Devi," a great devotee of Lord Krishna. Tulasi Devi was granted a boon by the Lord to remain in His presence eternally as a sacred Tulasi plant in his celestial abode.

Annai's favourite means of worship, is to worship the feet of her Lord, Babaji, in a ceremony known as "Pada Poosai." "Pada" means "feet" and "poosai" means to worship with flowers. During this ceremony, she lovingly places the feet of Babaji on a silver plate, washes and anoints them with sesame oil, mung bean powder, milk and other fragrances or precious articles. She then adorns his feet with "vibhuti" (ash from the mantra yagna fire), "kumkuma" (a red powder from the vermilion flower), and a number of other flowers growing in the ashram. (...) Among the disciples of Babaji, only Amman and Annai have attained the deathless state of soruba samadhi. Their attainment, more than anything, reflects the completeness of their self surrender to God, the highest goal of Kriya Yoga."[2]

The *sadhana* of Mataji

"Having overcome the limitations of the ego-consciousness, they now assist all who seek their aid. Annai, in particular, assists Kriya Yoga sadhakas during the midnight meditation hour to completely cleanse the subconscious mind using the first meditation technique taught during the initiation into Kriya

Dhyana Yoga."[3] This is known as "the sadhana (spiritual practice) of Annai," a practice of meditation and mantras which is realized between 11:45 pm and 12:45 am.

The purification of the subconscious mind or "chitta" is a key point for the spiritual realization. According to some authors, the word "siddha" derives from the word *"cittar"* (pronounced "siddhar") in Tamil. A Siddha would be someone who is a master of consciousness, one who has purified his chitta or subconscious mind.

The practice of the first meditation technique, Shuddi, at that moment, is very beneficial, as at that hour close to sleep the subconscious its activated, and their contents appears to the surface, so they can be cleaned. Also, this practice impresses in the mind the pattern of detachment, which is useful to have a restful sleep when we fall in its unconsciousness. And lastly, it is a good moment to experience the grace of Mataji, the Divine Mother.

1- *The Voice of Babaji.* p.14.
2- Govindan, M. (1993). *Babaji and the 18 Siddha Kriya Yoga tradition.* St. Etienne de Bolton, Quebec: Babaji's Kriya Yoga and Publications. p.81-83.
3- Id., p.83.

Mantras: tuning to higher frequencies

Mantras or divine sounds are syllables that, through repetition, have the power of creating in the student a higher state of energy and consciousness. Mantras are transmitted by masters with spiritual realization; these masters themselves received them from a higher consciousness or their own masters. And they knew that by giving them to their students, a similar consciousness could be realized.

Underlying a mantra is an elevated energy, but too, a higher state of consciousness is potentially hidden within it, like the potential tree lies in a tiny seed. Constant repetition of the mantra with dedication and devotion will cause the seed to germinate into a big tree, a great state of divine consciousness and energy: *"Then Jesus asked, 'What is the kingdom of God like? What shall I compare it to? It is like a mustard seed, which a man took and planted in his garden. It grew and became a tree, and the birds perched in its branches'"* (Luke 13.18-19).

Mantras are not learned in books, but received through a spiritual lineage that dates back to a spiritual realized yogi – this lineage preserves the spiritual power of the mantra. The act of receiving the mantra is called "initiation." There are, although, some mantras so extremely powerful that its repetition doesn't require a previous initiation, like the mantra "Om Namah Shivaya."

The continuous repetition of the mantra allows the concentration of all disperse thoughts, focusing the mind in a single point. This is a form of meditation, a dynamic form, which with practice, can be incorporated to the ordinary activities of the daily life: cleaning, driving the car, washing, etc., so transforming these activities in Karma Yoga, action offered to the Divine.

Different aspects of the Divine

In the poems of the Siddhas, which offer yogic teachings in a veiled way, we can read several invocations to the gods: Shiva, Ganesha, Muruga... The Siddhas were not polytheists. Nowhere in their writings do they sing praises to any gods or goddesses. But they did characterize sometimes divine qualities or powers with their names, associating these, especially with the chakras. Their approach is eminently practical, not theological. In the different phases of the spiritual evolution, or working with different chakras, the student would need to invocate different aspects of the Higher Consciousness, according the needs of the moment, with his own personal devotion.

In Babaji's Kriya Yoga the student can receive the mantras of the different divine qualities and powers, which are sometimes personified in different gods and goddesses. Goddess Durga, by example, represented with many arms with weapons, riding a lion, is the manifestation of the Divine that helps you in the elimination of the negative karma of the past; she also represents the gradual and disciplined rise of Kundalini energy.

Each one of the 18 Siddhas of Kriya Yoga tradition has a mantra; through these mantras the student can contact them. Babaji and Mataji also have their own mantras.

The constant concentration in the mantra allows the student to stop the mental dispersion and concentrating the mind and the energies in one divine aspect. This attunement is a continuous source of inspiration, of discernment, and with the adequate practice, of bliss.

The power of the Name

One of the more immediate ways of connecting with Babaji is through the repetition of the mantra "Om Kriya Babaji Nama Aum." Many of the realized yogis of India of recent times have praised the power of the repetition of the divine name. The *Vishnu Purana* says:

Kaliyug is the mine of faults, but it has only one great virtue - that the people will acquire divine position only by reciting Lord's name. Recitation of Lord's name, regardless of intention and motivation-- whether it is love, derision, laziness or maliceness- would destroy one's sins. But the sinister people would do even the most difficult tasks in Kaliyug, but they would not recite Lord's name. They would not have an interest in the Lord. Their interests would be more in sensuous things like sound, touch, beauty, scent etc. The Paramgati (supreme salvation) that people could receive by ten thousand years of meditation in Satayug; by performing Yagya for hundred years in Tretayug and by worshipping Lord's idol for ten years in Dwapar, that supreme salvation is easily available for people in Kaliyug simply by reciting Lord's name for one day and one night continuously. But still, in Kaliyug people would not have faith in Lord's name. It is their misfortune. [1]

In "The Voice of Babaji" we can also find these quotes about the mantra "Om Kriya Babaji Nama Aum":

You may do japa (repetition of a mantra) of 'Om Kriya Babaji Nama Aum.' That is a very powerful mantra. None can explain the benefits of japa, sadhana and satsanga. Japa is the rod in the hands of the blind sadhakas to plod on the road to realization. Japa is the philosopher's stone or divine elixir that makes one god-like. (…) May you have unshakable faiths in the miraculous powers and marvelous benefits of 'Om Kriya Babaji Nama Aum!' May you all realize the glory of Babaji- the name of God Himself! [2]

The recital of the mantra 'Om Kriya Babaji Nama Aum,' for instance destroys your sins and brings everlasting peace, infinite bliss, prosperity and immortality. There is not the least doubt about this. [3]

You should have perfect faith in Babaji's name, His grace and mercy.[4]

Meaning of Om Kriya Babaji Nama Aum

The syllables of a mantra can be "bija" or seed sounds, which have the power of activating particular potential powers or energies in the student who repeats them. Apart from these "bija" syllables which do not have an intellectual meaning, there are other words in the mantra which do while reflecting on their meaning, the effect is greater, and helps to manifest within oneself the quality associated with the mantra.

With this goal, I'm going to explain the meaning of the words of the mantra "Om Kriya Babaji Nama Aum." "Om Kriya Babaji Nama Aum" can be chanted aloud, or silently, to invoke the grace of the master of the Himalayas. "And who is Babaji?" we may ask. Maybe we could infer it through His mantra:

Om – Aum

Om represents the sound of the universe as we experience it externally, and *Aum* as it is experienced internally.

Aum is composed of three letters, which represent the three states of consciousness that we experience: waking, dreaming and dreamless sleep. Beyond these three states there is a fourth state, which corresponds with the silence that remains after the pronunciation of "Aum": the state of "turiya," the source of the others. It is the state of unity and enlightenment which sustains everything, beyond the changes and the impermanence inside and outside of us.

In the *Aum* symbol we can see these three states, and the dot, beyond the changing creation, represents this fourth state of enlightenment:

Om would be the cosmic roar of the universe, available to the yogi through the practice of some special techniques.

So we can see here the transition from the cosmic multiplicity of the universe to the absolute monism of the One, from the roar of form to the perfect silence of the Self: from *Om* to *Aum*. From multiplicity to unity.

This is shown also in Babaji's yantra (yantras are visual symbols used to meditate in a divine aspect): the outer circle represents the macrocosms, and the central dot represents the only Self, the center of everything.

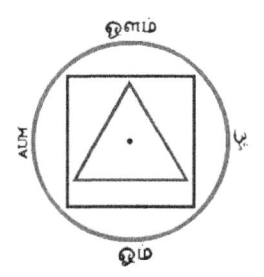

Kriya

"Kriya," or action with consciousness, would be a form of invocating the principles of Shiva and Shakti, of uniting matter and Spirit, of invoking the perfect synthesis of both. This is the realization of Babaji and the Siddhas, who do not renounce the world, but seek the descent of Divinity within it, perfecting it.

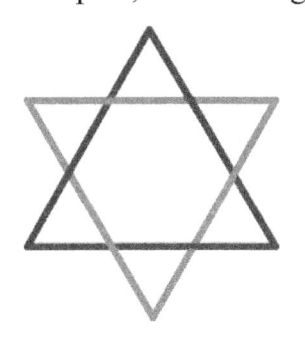

This perfect synthesis of matter and Spirit, of the Divine and the form, is represented by the six pointed star, symbol of the unions of Shiva (triangle that points upwards) with Shakti (the triangle that points downwards). It is a symbol that we can find in the images of the Siddhas.

Babaji

This is the name of the living source of Kriya Yoga. How can be defined Babaji? For Yogi Ramaiah, teacher of Marshall Govindan Satchidananda, Babaji is an incarnation of Lord Muruga, one of the favorite personifications of the Lord among of the Siddhas of the South of India. Lord Muruga, son of Shiva, is represented a youth carrying spear, the *vel*, which represents fully awakened kundalini, the ultimate weapon for overcoming the darkness of ignorance. It is said that he was born from the third eye of Shiva, as a ray of light.

Muruga

According to the legendary *Skanda Puranas,* Lord Muruga left Mount Kailash in Tibet, the residence of Shiva, and settled down in Katargama, Sri Lanka, where he married Valli, the daughter of an aboriginal chieftain. In Lord Muruga we find that the Divine descends from inhospitable and elevated regions, far from what we can conceive, to the most ordinary daily lif.

This descent is what we call "grace." Grace is a descent of the divine blessing, deserved or not, beyond our logic and comprehension, which transforms the devotee.

In Lord Muruga we find the attributes of eternal youth, of

light and of the descent of grace.

It is said that Babaji Nagaraj attained "soruba samadhi," the divinization even of the physical body, when He was 16 years old. In the text of the Siddhas, the decisive role of the divine light and grace is repeatedly described.

So, by invoking Babaji through His name, we are invoking the personification of divine grace and light which can destroy darkness and ignorance which are the source of all suffering.

Nama

It means "salutation" or "I bow to."

The goal of Babaji and the 18 Siddhas is "complete surrender" of the egoistic perspective to the perspective of our soul, the Eternal Witness. This occurs as a result of one's aspiration, or call, and the response or grace of the Lord. Anyone, regardless of circumstances and belief, can invoke this grace through the repetition of the name "Om Kriya Babaji Nama Aum." As Yogi Ramiah often said: "Take one step towards Babaji, and He takes ten steps towards you;" and "Seek Babaji to become Babaji."

From what we have said, we can see that through this mantra we invoke the descent of the divine light and grace for a perfect realization of the Spirit in the matter, the realization of the One in all the diversity. We invoke the personification and the perfect realization of all this.

1- Hindu Online: *Vishnu Purana.* Disponible en http://hinduonline.co/
2- *The Voice of Babaji*, p.431.
3- Id., p.456.
4- Id., p.480.

The Tantra of the 18 Siddhas

A practical and short definition of Tantra is: the effort of concentrating in the higher *chakras*, in the top of the head, the vital energy that is accumulated in the lower *chakras*. By doing so, it is this energy by itself that activates the most elevated states of consciousness, associated with the higher *chakras*.

The transmutation of sexual energy into spiritual energy is one of the key points emphasized by the Siddhas in their writings. Among them stands out the texts of the Siddha Boganathar, who is said to be the founder of Taoism, a discipline that specializes in the transmutation of this energy.

To be able to transmute this energy successfully we must take into account the different components of our subtle anatomy, what is present in the vital body, the energetic body that supports and sustains our physical body, which is also the seat of our desires and emotions. These components are the *nadis* or energy channels and the *chakras* or centers of energy and consciousness. Both must be purified and activated through various yogic practices including asanas, pranayama, mantras and particular meditation techniques.

The energetic system of the vital body can be compared with an electric circuit, with its different electric cables (*nadis*) and batteries (*chakras*), through which our life force, known as *prana,* circulates. The less purified the cables and the batteries are, the more resistance they will offer to the passing of the energy, so the circuit will be overheated, and will only tolerate reduced voltages of electricity; it won't stand high levels of energy. A whole range of desires and emotions leave a residue in our subtle anatomy, which accumulates and creates energetic blockages in the *nadis* and *chakras*.

An unusual inner experience, motivated by a transmission of energy (what some call "*Shaktipat*") or by an intensive but unbalanced practice, can result in a great discharge of electricity in the circuit. But if it is not ready to withstand this voltage, there will be a spark, a short circuit that could damage some of its components. Some people value these as "spiritual experiences" because of their sometimes dramatic or sensational effects. But such experiences have no intrinsic value; nor do they last. They are really indications of our lack of preparation. So, our work as students of Yoga is to set up an inner electric circuit that could withstand, in a steady a progressive way, higher and higher levels of energy – higher and higher levels of consciousness. This means a long term, constant and sustained effort, not a search for dramatic, energetic, or spiritual experiences.

The Siddhas of South India emphasize in their works the required spiritual work with the *chakras*, the *nadis* and with the *Kundalini*, which they describe as our potential power and consciousness, dormant in the first *chakra*, coincident with the perineum in men and just inside the vagina in women.

Kriyas (techniques) of Yoga

In Babaji's Kriya Yoga we have the fundamental practice of the 18 asanas to purify the *nadis* and to gradually activate the *chakras*. Yogis such as Swami Satyananda Saraswati point out the importance of activating the *chakras* in a gradual and progressive way, as their sudden opening may overwhelm the practitioner with desires and uncontrollable emotions, when deep seated habitual desires and emotions, are activated too quickly.

To avoid such problems, we practice the first mediation technique, *Shuddi Dhyana Kriya*, to cleanse the subconscious mind, where undesirable habits and tendencies (*samskaras* and *vasanas*) are stored. Also, in the third initiation, we learn some advanced meditation techniques to complete this purification, like the Divine Openings meditations and others. The repetition of *mantras* can also be effective for this purification of the subconscious.

Other essential techniques to activate the *chakras* and transmute the vital/sexual energy are:

- *Bandahs* or muscular locks – the Siddha Tirumular speaks about these practices in his work "Tirumandiram"; several texts of Yoga like "*Hatha Yoga Pradipika*" emphasize also these techniques.

- The pranayamas *Brahmacharya Ojas Matreika Pranayama* and *Kriya Kundalini Pranayama*.

In the third initiation we also learn kriyas or specific techniques to activate the *chakras* and to purify their contents, through meditations, *mantras* and *asanas*.

The Light and Grace of the Divine

The concept of "Grace," the descent of divine energy and consciousness, is very present in the tradition of the Siddhas (called *Saiva Siddhantam* of the South of India). *Shiva*, the Divine itself, the Absolute, is a term that means "auspiciousness" or "goodness." In the book "Tirumandiram," Tirumular mentions five actions of *Shiva*, the Godhead: creation, preservation, destruction, obscuration and grace, and all these actions are considered acts of grace and love by the Lord for the souls, enabling them to consciously reunite with it in beatitude

In response to the efforts by the yogi to prepare and purify himself or herself for reuniting ("yoga") with the Divine, and through the yogi's continuous call and surrender of the egoistic perspective to that of the soul, our Witness-consciousness, Grace descends, as supporting strength and inner guidance.

This yogic effort includes the accumulation of vital energy in the higher centers of consciousness or *chakras*. This is attained not only with yogic techniques, but also with sustained devotion and aspiration, and with a right and ethical behavior. All these allow the vision of the divine Light. This light of consciousness is constantly mentioned in the *Tirumandiram* and in other poems of the Siddhas:

*If one concentrates on the form of light, there is illumination;
If one melts in the light, He will become one with you.*

- Tirumandiram 2681[1]

*Like the drops of water that will not adhere to the leaf of the lotus
such is the desire of the world
Push it away leave it and
worship and adore o dancing snake
the feet of the dazzling
blazing brilliant white light
shining everywhere.*

- Siddha Pambatti[2]

*O praise the Light of the Lamp, the jewel of the skies,
the great light of reflection, the jewel in the eye!
O praise the Light with rays which have transgressed the
 trinity of time
and hold it firm within your heart and mind!*

- Siddha Idai Kadar[3]

*To those who have known
that the Truth is plain Light,
what is the use of royal grants?*

Siddha Kudambai[4]

The Siddha Tirumular also mentions the hearing of the *Nada*, the primordial vibration underlying everything, and referred to as AUM, or OM, as result of this concentration of vital energy in the higher *chakras*. The yogic discipline or *sadhana* brings about the union of *Bindu* and *Nada* – the union of the vital/sexual seed energy with the Om, the union of the individualized consciousness with the universal consciousness, first manifesting as AUM.

In Classical Yoga, as expounded in the *Yoga-Sutras* of Patanjali, the goal is the attainment of *Nirvikalpa Samadhi*, the merging of the individualized consciousness into the absolute, pure consciousness, with the result of *Moksha* or liberation of the individual from the compulsory cycle of reincarnation.

In the wisdom teachings of the Siddhas, known as *Saiva Siddhantam*, the goal of the *Soruba Samadhi*, includes the descent of Divinity into all five planes of existence, an integral transformation of our human nature into a Divine Being. Rather than seeking to escape from this world of suffering the Siddhas, sought perfection, *"siddhi,"* the full expression of our Divine potential, with the perfect union of *Shiva* an *Shakti* in the human being, the transmutation of matter (which is energy, after all) in the perfect expression of the Divine consciousness.

To this attainment, the divine Light is, now, the divine principle intermediate between the Absolute and the creation, participating in both. This principle would be the transmuting agent of this process, being able to act even on the physical body:

If concentrating on the light and chanting clearly
With a melting light, (He will) make the body
A golden one by the alchemic pill of Sivaya Nama.

– Tirumandiram 2709

A Siddha of the 19th century, Ramalinga spoke about all this in his many poems, where he invokes the Divine in its aspect of "divine Light of Grace" (*Arul Perun Jyoti*), so It could descend and transmute the physical body into an immortal body of light. He himself attained this final yogic realization; nevertheless his message didn't have much receptivity in his contemporaries.

But this descent of the divine Grace in the form of light belongs to advanced phases of the *sadhana*, once all the requisites mentioned above have been accomplished.

To these previous requisites we must add a total surrender to the Divine. An aspect emphasized by modern Siddhas like Sri Aurobindo and the Mother. Their Integral Yoga, which also points to a total transformation, including the physical, starts and ends with this complete surrender to the Divine, in its dynamic and energetic aspect: the Divine Mother.

The role of the guru

The Siddhas stress also the role of the *guru* who prescribes a *sadhana*, a specific spiritual practice for the disciple to follow, and with Divine grace completes the process of spiritual realization, the union with the Divine. This is made possible when the disciple follows the prescribed sadhana and surrenders egoism. The *guru* is that which comes through the Self-realized teacher: the teachings, which in turn reveal Truth, Love, Beauty, and Wisdom. The guru is therefore a necessary doorway to the Divine, the Absolute according to the teachings of the Siddhas.

The spiritual approach of the Siddhas is direct, practical and realist, beyond theological speculation. The student will advance on the path as long as he dedicates himself to the prescribed yogic practice, with faith and devotion to the sadhana, the guru and to the Divine. The happiness of the student will be proportional to his or her self-discipline, or *sadhana*.

The Siddhas declare also that the divine Grace is always

being poured upon us, like rain, but through yogic *sadhana* we learn to become vessels, able to receive and collect it, without any fissures. *Shiva*, the Divine, is the quintessence, the endless source of this Grace.

1- Tirumular Siddhar. (2010). *The Tirumandiram*. Volume 9. St. Etienne de Bolton, Québec: Babaji's Kriya Yoga and Publications.
2- V. Zvelebil, Kamil.(1993). *The poets of the Powers*. California: Integral Publishing. p. 117.
3- Id., p. 108.
4- Id., p. 111.

Recovering the Self

The self is the friend of the Self, for him who has conquered himself by this Self. But to the unconquered self, this self is inimical, and behaves like an external foe.

To the self-controlled and serene, the Supreme Self is, the object of constant, realization, in cold and heat, pleasure and pain, as well as in honor and dishonor, Bhagavad Gita, VI.6-7.

In our process of growth and transformation which is Yoga, it is very useful, to be happy, to remember and to have in mind who truly are we, and who we are not. Yoga teaches that we are the Seer, an unconditional and blissful watcher, who in our immediate experience is surrounded by a mental body, an emotional body and a physical body: thoughts, feelings and sensations. These three are changing and impermanent, with different degrees of density: mind is volatile and changes with a dizzying speed; emotions are denser more difficult more difficult to change, once they are activated; and lastly, it takes a certain effort to move the physical body.

We must remember that:

- Behind the mind, behind each thought, there is pure consciousness.

- Behind each emotion there is peace and bliss.

All thoughts and emotions are transitory, They are not the Self, but our creation.

The waves of thoughts and emotions cover the pure consciousness, and the peace and bliss of our original and real nature.

Nevertheless, we can't reject the thoughts and the emotions trying to experience peace and bliss all the time, because this will create a duality in us, we divide ourselves trying to fight against ourselves. And we can hardly live without thoughts and feelings, because even if we could (so to say) eliminate them in ourselves, we'll still experience the thoughts and the feelings of those around us.

The yogi, instead of that, embraces everything that surrounds him, accepting everything with full awareness. The Seer, the witness, is eternal, but thoughts and feelings are not. Full awareness, full consciousness accepts everything that appears, but doesn't cling to anything. In reality every phenomenon is born in it, manifests in it, and finally, when the original impulse is exhausted, gets dissolved in it.

A legend from India narrates that when the goddess Kali (the divine energy that destroys all negativity) slew the demons, she started to dance frenetically, and it seemed that the entire universe was going to be destroyed also. To avoid this, the god Shiva, her consort, laid down at her feet. Kali stopped her dance, in shame, when she found out that she was dancing over her husband.

In a similar way, pure consciousness (Shiva) dissolves into itself every manifestation of energy (Shakti or Kali). The witness in us is Shiva, our eternal and indestructible Self.

The stains of our human nature

There are several "stains" known as *malas* in our human nature: ignorance, egoism, karma and delusion prevent us from remaining in a state of Self realization. Karma is the sum of our habits and tendencies. Delusion, or maya, is the confusion created by attachments and aversions. These accumulate throughout our lives. Some are quite evident, but others are more subtle and hidden. The yogi must confront each of these formations, one after another, in his daily work, until finally he is even confronting collective blocks, common to all his society, like social tendencies or fears. And if the yogi persists in his spiritual discipline, he confronts the basic stain, ignorance of

Self, that create his own ego, the main rock, the belief that he is an isolated individual, a set of individual thoughts, feelings and perceptions, instead of the blissful consciousness, unconditional and unconditioned.

To clean these formations that nurture the ego and hide the Self, we must:

- First, find out the mental and emotional habits that nurture and support them, like holes that drain the energy that, otherwise, we would use for the purposes of the Self. These habits could be our usual fears and worries, anger, stress, unsatisfied desires, dissatisfaction, etc.

- Later we must accept and transform the "karmic residues" that remain there: see them, accept them, understand them, offer them to the Divine and release them.

With the release of all the mind stuff, the student could experience an uncomfortable feeling of emptiness, which is yet another creation to be released. One only becomes at ease with emptiness and aloneness through devotion to the Self and the satguru and surrender to one's path of growth.

The student could also feel fear for his/her own annihilation – another creation that has nothing to do with the Self. Fear is one of the basic formations of the ego; it bases on fear its different and aberrant vital strategies. Even living without fear is fearful to the ego.

Integrating the emotions without repressing them is an art, the same as observing and understanding one's own thoughts without being carried away by them. This is made possible with the cultivation of consciousness and full awareness. Different techniques of Kriya Yoga help us with this; we must remember that "Kriya" means "action with awareness." We then discover in our practice that the real Yoga is not limited to a meditation session, but to the constant cultivation of awareness and equanimity. Our Yoga is our life, a chance of living the Self in the middle of our experiences. Each challenge to our equanimity is a chance to practice our Yoga. There is not a single moment in our life when we can't develop our practice of Yoga!

The Yoga of emotions

The student of Yoga learns to quiet the mind, to observe and stop the thoughts, entering in a space of calmness and serenity.

But, as one advances in the path, even when thoughts have departed, one notices the presence of deep seated emotions. This happens especially if one follows a deep and transforming Yoga (the real Yoga, indeed), where powerful energies are mobilized, which activate the contents of the subconscious mind. These contents can come to the light of consciousness, without any other objective that being uprooted from the psyche. The Kundalini energy, for example, works like this, activating the stored impressions and tendencies (*samskaras* and *vasanas*) in the background of our mind.

For this reason Patanjali defines Yoga as *"the cessation of the (identification with) the modifications arising from the subconscious"* (Yoga Sutras I.2). Until this is attained, there is a long process of inner cleaning, and a great part of it is the dealing with emotions – the energetic contents of our *"pranamaya kosha"* or vital, emotional body, the second sheath of the Self after the physical body.

The adequate management of emotions is an art in Yoga, an art quite difficult to master. The Siddhas and the Yoga masters give us some suggestions about this matter.

The emotional limits of the "I"

If anyone asks me, I would say that the ego – our identification with the little "self" that we think we are – is basically emotional, not mental. The bonds that tie us with our little "I" are mostly emotional. Who, for example, enjoys being alone all the time? The vital body has some very imperative needs, which are not transcended until the full realization of the Self.

The Witness, the Self that we really are, is characterized by its calmness and bliss. So, we know that these two traits, calmness and bliss, are of our real Self. The seat of our emotions is our vital body.

In Babaji's Kriya Yoga one learns to develop the perspective of the witness towards the emotions. In Babaji's Kriya Yoga one learns to develop the perspective of the witness towards the emotions. This means accepting each one of them unconditionally, while at the same time, attaching to none.

The yogi looks for the expansion of consciousness, not its contraction. Some people practice Yoga with the same attitude of someone who smokes hashish or drinks whisky – just to disconnect from their conflicting emotions that need to be healed. Yoga doesn't try to disconnect us from everything. On the contrary, its goal is to connect us with everything, uniting our individual consciousness with the cosmic consciousness, our true home. Yoga doesn't try to disconnect from anything except egoism, the habit of contraction, of identifying with what we are not. On the contrary, its goal is to connect with everything, uniting our little consciousness with the cosmic consciousness, our true home.

Therefore, practicing Yoga to avoid negative feelings or to become settled in some perpetual "good vibe," (something that life won't allow for long anyway) will limit your growth. Yoga is meant to expand the consciousness, embracing everything with it, to overcome every personal limitation. To expand ourselves, we must all, sooner or later, jump over the fence of egoism, ignoring the "No trespass" warning, to enter into transpersonal space.

If students feel overwhelmed by their own emotions, they must imagine what it would feel like to, all at once, experience the collective emotions of everyone around them – what the masters called "cosmic consciousness…" a terrible thing, isn't? For this reason we must master the art of "detachment" or *vairagya*.

When emotions dance

Through the art of detachment we learn to observe our emotions without repressing them, but without encouraging them. We only observe them, without any thought about them. We release them to the light of consciousness. In this way, they lose their own drive, just as raindrops stop, when the rain is over. The Self is eternal and omnipresent, but emotions are not. So, from the perspective of the Self, our resources of awareness are infinite.

That is basically detachment, rightly practiced, without repression: a pure awareness that accepts and perceives everything but doesn't cling to anything, even to the act of not clinging. Something easy to understand, but it takes a lifetime of practice to master.

It seems easy, but in the practice, certainly it isn't. In fact, we all have some basic emotions that we are not ready to feel, under no circumstances, because they are so painful for our ego (which was formed with them) that we think that we will die if we experience them again. And we have organized our personality and our life not to feel them again (we could even practice Yoga with this goal).

Some therapies that facilitate the release of deep conflictive emotions could be very useful. But all them, finally, must apply the principle of detachment, rightly practiced: bringing all the conflicts in one's personal image into the light, to be accepted and released. It requires letting go.

The student who truly advances in Yoga is able to eliminate inner mental barriers and liberate deeply-held emotional content stored in the subconscious, perhaps even over several lifetimes. When heavy content come up, it can be overwhelming, and in that moment one could ask "Why is this happening to me, I was happy in my ignorance, where I am going?" This is the real Yoga – the one which transforms you! The Mother, of Sri Aurobindo Ashram, said that once you enter into Yoga, it is better to go on until the end; you can't let things half-done…

Maybe it sounds scary, but we must consider that not advancing, not transforming ourselves may be a painful waste of a lifetime– in the long term. Being irremediably stuck in the same limiting subconscious stuff causes stagnation of body, mind and spirit and leads us only unpleasantly into old age. *"A minimum of practice of this Yoga will let you off countless suffering after death"* says Krishna in the Bhagavad Gita. And moreover, it will let you experience levels of bliss that – as Sri Aurobindo said – we can't even now conceive that exist. So the effort in Yoga is worthwhile, even a minimum of it.

The constant practice of the witness and detachment helps with emotional purification, as if one is bailing water out of the boat he/she is sailing. But another positively, active way of emotional purification is to cultivation of the habit of being at ease, content and emotionally, at peace. Sri Aurobindo recommends this: *"If you get peace, then to clean the vital becomes easy. If you simply clean and clean and clean and do nothing else, you go very slowly – for the vital gets dirty again and has to be cleaned a hundred times. The peace is something that is clean in itself, so to get it is a positive way of securing your object. To look for dirt only and clean is the negative way."*

The final goal of the process, a great triumph for the yogi, is to make the vital body absolutely transparent, without densities that could obstruct the descent of light from the higher centers of consciousness. A vital body that surrenders to the higher purposes of these spiritual centers provides ever-abundant energy. This is, certainly, the true alchemy, the most elevated one.

Emotional basis for peace

The stillness lies in surrender of all things and the Spirit is fain for the stillness, Kriya Babaji.

Bliss, *ananda*, is one of the goals of Yoga. The experience shows that, in the practice of Yoga, first there appears peace, and from this, there appears the divine bliss, the bliss of the Self, called "ananda." This bliss doesn't depend upon the fickle emotional body, but upon the deeper identification with the real Self, attained through the yogic practices.

A steady and permanent bliss can only exist in a steady and permanent basis of peace. And, certainly, usually the emotional body doesn't help so much to get this.

Society also doesn't really favor our peace; it is constantly driving us to buy and consume more – or to earn money to do that. But at the end of this endless process, it is not us who are finally consumed? To attain peace, what does society offers us? Normally, it is pills.

How can we create a basis of peace inside us, to build our realization of the bliss of the Self?

There are different values and attitudes in Yoga, apart from the specific yogic techniques, that I have found very useful and valuable for my yogic practice and for my life. I'm going to mention some of them. These attitudes are for me a foundation for the yogic sadhana, the spiritual disciple, as the make possible, or at least they favor the inner peace. Their observance is another discipline, until they became a habit, a second nature. But the final result makes the effort worthwhile enough.

These attitudes are the witness consciousness, discernment and surrender.

The witness consciousness

We all have an ego, our belief in the separated existence, which is ultimately based on basic emotions to survive. Our real Self doesn't need to survive, is eternal, but our body and its biological instincts have developed strategies to preserve the life of its cells along thousands of years.

Our ego develops strategies of interchange with the world, especially in the social relationships, to get from others the things that we think we need to survive: nutrition, attention, recognition, etc. Each individual develops different strategies to "survive," consciously or unconsciously, but the aims are quite similar.

In Yoga we learn to develop the consciousness of the witness as an antidote towards the identification with the basic tendencies of our human nature. In this way we find a point of stability in front of the ups and downs of life. The basic norm would be: "Observe and notice everything, but don't take anything personally."

It is exhausting to try to constantly uphold the self-esteem of an ego, because its existence is truly based in perpetual wounds to its self-esteem. Is like investing money in a bottomless hole. As we find peace and plenitude inside ourselves through the practice of Yoga, we stop demanding others and the world to give us what we think that we don't have and we need, and we can start giving unconditionally.

Some psychologists speak much about connecting with the "inner child," but it is equally necessary or more to connect with the "inner mother." A child only thinks in receiving, he requires someone to give him their constant attention. A mother gives unconditionally. We could nurture our inner child to make him grow and become a mother. Consequently he will become full enough of all the things he cried for (attention, love, nutrition), to the extent of giving them freely to others.

Let us imagine two men walking on the street: a beggar, asking money from everyone he meets, and a rich man, giving money to everyone he meets. Which one of them will attract more people? Everyone will flee from the beggar, while the rich man will be surrounded by people. Similarly, we can go through life demanding love and attention, or offering them to everyone. To receive both things you only have to give them freely.

We can apply the consciousness of the witness to everything around us, but, mostly, to ourselves. By doing so we could identify the games and strategies of our ego in our relationships with the world. And we can give up these games, because we know that finally we never win in them.

With the consciousness of the witness we can discover our unconscious games, the shell of our ego. Then, we take a breath, we can relax and smile. We already have all that this ego is looking for, in our limitless peace of Yoga. We only need to release and relax enough to realize it.

Discernment

The vision of discernment is seeing the Divine in everything. By doing so we are not trapped by duality: good and bad, right or wrong, light and darkness. The dual vision enslaves us to suffering, perpetually trying to run away from "evil" and constantly running after the "good." You don't come out from duality; it is the basis of hate, one of the most tenacious obstacles to our spiritual growth.

An example of something extremely opposed to discernment is the "tribal principle," based on duality, which we can see in many forms around us: nationalisms, political ideologies, local rivalries, sport rivalries. It is based in the idea that there is "another" who is different from us. By the psychological mechanism of projection, we eventually see in the other everything that we dislike or repress in ourselves: our shadow. This is exactly opposed to the process of personal integration that requires our growth to "samadhi" or the experience of full unity.

We all have been hurt by someone at some moment in our

life, sometimes in a totally unjustified or undeserved way. It is human nature in these cases to hate. The vision of discernment can be difficult, but it liberates us from harboring hate. We all have pending karmic consequences for things that we did in the past, or due to a lack of learning in this life. The karmic lesson is a way of learning and evolving, sometimes in quite a dramatic way, but, because of this, it is very useful and effective.

It can be useful to feel that forgiving a great offense is a means of forgiving ourselves for the same offense, committed in the past. Or, another method would be to ask ourselves: "What do I have to learn from this situation?"

The book "The Voice of Babaji" dedicates one chapter to the vision of discernment:

Behold that Light shining in every form and face. Learn to recognize the unmistakable Presence in every phenomenon. One who always lives this way never strays away from the right, from dharma. He never loses the sight of the Truth. He never fails into darkness. [1]

The final practice of Bhakti Yoga, the Yoga of devotion, is this: seeing the Divine in everything. Krishna says it clearly in the Bhagavad Gita (VI.29-31):

With the mind harmonized by Yoga, he (the yogi) sees the Self abiding in all beings and all beings in the Self; he sees the same everywhere.

He who sees Me everywhere and sees everything in Me never becomes separated from Me, nor do I become separated from him.

He who is established in unity worships Me who dwells in all beings, that yogi abides in Me, whatever may be his mode of living.

This is the vision of the *bhakti yogi*, who follows the path of devotion, and also of the *jnana yogi*, who follows the path of wisdom: seeing the One in everything. And this is the real view, the view of the Self-realize human.

Surrender

Surrender is attunement and constant opening to a higher power (the Divine, en any chosen form), seeing everything that happens as coming from the Divine, and surrendering the results of everything – and the future – to that power.

Probably it could be the most difficult quality to achieve. Surrender is the most important value in the path of the Siddhas, which makes possible the final realization of *soruba samadhi*, the final goal mentioned by the Siddhas. Truly, all Yoga is a process of surrender to our Higher Consciousness. Finally one ends surrendering one's own preferences (the attachments and aversion of the emotional body).

Surrender is the radical basis of peace. "The stillness lies in surrender of all things" and the spirit is fain for the stillness" says Babaji, the same as the poet Dante says in his "Divine Comedy": "Our peace in His will."

Surrender allows us to release the strategies of the ego, as we realize more and more that our survival doesn't depend upon us as we believed before... We are not even responsible of the breathing of our body or the beaten of our hearts. We can always improve our life with our effort (depending more or less of our karmic credit), but just to some extent.

Surrender is based in the constant attunement with a higher power. And, as Sri Aurobindo and the Mother teach again and again, this higher power can act through us and our life, in the same measure that we are constantly open to it.

Openness in work means the same thing as openness in the consciousness. The same Force that works in your consciousness in meditation and clears away the cloud and confusion whenever you open to it, can also take up your action and not only make you aware of the defects in it but keep you conscious of what is to be done and guide your mind and hands to do it.[2]

In their Integral Yoga of Sri Aurobindo and the Mother they didn't teach yogic techniques but rather the constant opening to the power of the Divine. And certainly, their ashram, managed by the Mother, housed around 2,000 disciples, donor-supported, even in times of war. One could conclude that the Divine, without the interferences of the ego, is naturally prosperous!

Affirmations

Yoga teaches – and one can discover it through practice – that the Divine is always there, an omnipresent Presence; but He is "in silence," beyond the noisy world that the ego creates inside and outside us. So we will only start perceiving Him when we stop our identification with the noise inside and outside us.

The ego (and the society created by it) is scared by silence, and constantly tries to fill it with noise and with "things." It constantly tries to run away from the emptiness and "loneliness" that its own existence creates, based in the separation from everything. It takes courage to get out of this frenzy. Because living without fear is frightening!

Surrender is the antithesis of fear. The cultivation of the consciousness of the witness and of the discernment helps to develop surrender.

Our mind is constantly bombarded by negative messages. If we see the TV programs we'll see that, to win a larger audience, its programming appeals our basic instincts of sex and fear of survival. The other media doesn't offer a better alternative. It is important to choose those sources of information and entertainment that nurture our yogic practice and our spiritual aspirations.

The practice of affirmations using the Yoga Nidra technique (taught in the Second Initiation) can help to transform mental-emotional patterns of fear. It can be done in 21 consecutive days, engraving the affirmation in the mind until the change is attained. 21 days is the time, according to some psychologist, required to engrave the affirmation in the subconscious mind.

The famous "Serenity prayer" resumes pretty well the attitude of surrender:

God grant me the serenity
To accept the things I cannot change,
The courage to change the things I can,
And the wisdom to know the difference.

There are four points, inspired in the Bhagavad Gita, which resume what surrender is, and that I like to repeat frequently:

- Everything (I surrender) belongs to the Divine.
- The Divine is inside everyone, as the inner Self.
- I get free by following the will of the Divine.
- The bliss I'm looking for is, in reality, the bliss of the Divine.

The real Yoga starts when we start to introduce the consciousness of the witness, discernment and surrender in our life. Yoga is the transformation of our physical, emotional and mental vehicles in instruments for the manifestation of a Higher Consciousness, able to transcend radically the limitations that afflict us.

1- *The Voice of*, p. 241.
2- Aurobindo, Sri. (2003). *The integral Yoga*. Twin Lakes, USA: Lotus Press. p. 203.

The ego and the dance of Shiva

Many legends about the Hindu gods, gathered in the text called "Puranas," narrate the combats between them and the different demons that threaten the Earth and the heavens. Through these legends, the wise men of the past shared varied human and spiritual teachings. The fights against demons are metaphors of our inner processes of our fight for Self-realization, where we must defeat several enemies. The most important one of them is... our own "I," what we understand as "ego."

The Samkhya philosophical approach, in which Yoga is based, categorizes the different principles that constitute the reality of the universe, and the ego is one of these universal principles, responsible of out identification with a particular body and personality. In a practical sense, ego is translated as "me, myself and I," in the need of being special. This is a negative need, not from the moral point of view, but from the yogic point of view, because it prevents us enjoying our essence.

Babaji points out that the mind is the fortress of the ego. The diverse practices of Yoga are finally directed to destroy this fortress. The dragon of the ego (me, myself and I) hides and protects the treasure of our absolute existence-consciousness-bliss. To slay this dragon is not an easy task.

The image of Shiva Nataraj, dancing Shiva, can give us some clues to help us in this process. Because Shiva, apart from being the creator of Yoga, is the aspect of the Divine who destroy our ego, our lower self. As he dances, his right foot is on a demon, while his left foot is elevated upwards.

Shiva holds down the demon of the ego, but he doesn't try to annihilate him. If we try to slay our ego, we are dividing ourselves. And, by acting like this, we could create another ego, more subtle, as we will be proud of not having an ego. Instead of that, it will be enough for us to control egoism, to allow the underlying light of consciousness to influence our actions. A consistent practice of awareness allows us to see when egoism begins to guide our daily decisions and actions life. We will have "Aha, gotcha moments! There you are." Eventually the enormous energy we utilize to maintain our ego will finally be recovered by the Self. The world doesn't respect the ego of anyone, but prefers to finally crush them all.

The ego is like the tail of a tadpole, if you cut it, the tadpole dies. The tail will disappear by itself, with time, as long as the tadpole evolves into a frog. Our constant awareness and discernment allows us to stop nurturing this tail, this separation that truly keeps us away from our Self and from everything. Although this separation can for some time be of help to our growth. A stick in the soil will guide a small sprout upwards until it becomes strong and mature and if the stick is removed prematurely, the small sprout will not grow upwards and will never reach its potential.

The left foot of Shiva, pointing upwards the sky, suggests another way to overcome the ego: devotion. This is the sweetest food of the diverse yogic practices; it gives us the experience of love and bliss. But for this, one must be in love with the object of devotion. The so called "Ishta Devata" or personal concept of the Divine represents the individual form or conception of the Divine, the form used by the devotee to relate with the Divine. In India there are infinite forms of conceiving and relating with the Absolute, and this diversity is respected and promoted.

We can't force love, but we can cultivate it. In India the practice of yogic techniques is reduced to a minority of people, but many people follow many different devotional practices. They cultivate their relation with their Ishta Devata in all daily activities.

You can't take a bone from a dog, unless you offer him a bigger bone. By the same token, you can remove the tyranny of your ego unless you can surrender to something better. And love and devotion opens you to a sweeter surrender. Love and devotion has the power to dissolve the ego in the bliss of the beloved. The "me, myself and I" become secondary, after the "Thou, Thou." There is no effort in the process, no inner conflict.

Our Western culture is based in the cult of the ego, of being special, of being an "individual," and tries to silent our lack of inner bliss with consumerism and pills, without success, as we are realizing more and more. That is the reason why Yoga has so much to contribute to the West.

The practice of awareness and devotion, as Shiva suggests, helps us to subjugate the most misleading of demons, our little "I," allowing us to join in the bliss of the cosmic dance.

Integrated experiences – dissociated experiences

As Yoga teaches, in our subtle body we have seven psycho-energetic centers called "chakras," and each one of them is associated with a characteristic state of consciousness. Usually, unless we do anything to avoid it, our energy is concentrated in the first three chakras, so our habitual state of consciousness is associated with them. The first chakra is related with sexuality, the second with our basic survival, and the third one with the exertion of will and power to achieve our goals. It's no wonder, for example, that the sexual drive or the fears about survival are so predominant in our habitual consciousness or in our society (we only have to check the TV programs to confirm this). We know in Yoga that energy and consciousness are related; we try to bring our vital energy upwards, to the higher chakras, to experience the higher consciousness related with them.

In the spiritual marketplace some people are offering different ways to have dramatic openings and experiences – at least temporally – of the higher chakras, and moving spiritual experiences beyond ordinary consciousness. Through the consumption of drugs, natural ones or not, and the practice of some breathing techniques or intense and drastic meditations, this goal can be attained. Nevertheless, it must be pointed that although they offer a guarantee of some instant spiritual experience, appealing to our consumer society, the practices carry risks.

In Kriya Yoga and in other forms of Tantra, the chakras are activated and opened as the energy rises up in a gradual and progressive way, so the action of each chakra is supported by the chakras below. This keeps a balanced growth, where the yogi expands gradually his consciousness and his capacities, in harmony with his personality and his way of life. In Kriya Yoga, the different techniques, asanas, pranayamas, meditations, mantras, etc. work in synergy to this goal. Asanas, for example, clean the nadis or energy channels, easing the flow of energy between the chakras, without impediments; some meditation techniques clean the contents of the subconscious, which some say that are stored in the second chakras, and are a source of psychological disturbance for the individual.

A violent practice of pranayamas and determined meditation, the same as the consumption of drugs, can activate the experiences of the chakra of the forehead (related with "visions" of subtle planes, from the densest to the most subtle ones) or the chakra of the crown of the head (related with pure awareness, the non-dual state where there is no individual anymore). These experiences can have links with the activity of the lower chakras and the personality, or not. If there are not links, the result could be a fragmented consciousness between two experiences that cannot be united.

Let us imagine, by example, that a person experiences a temporal opening of the crown chakra, with its experience of the dissolution of the "I," and there is no energetic link between this chakra and the chakras below (barely activated), and the consciousness associated with the three first chakras. There will be difficulties when this person tries to integrate such experience with others in their life. This creates a sense of what Psychology calls "dissociation:" a split in the psyche. On one side is the experience of dissolution of the "I," and on the other, the ordinary experience of the individual, which will interpret the experience in its own way. It will possibly consider the experience a threat to its survival, and it will be a source of neurosis and mental disturbance.

It is useful, when we speak about the modified states of consciousness, to differentiate between two types of experiences:

- Experiences of fragmentation: those who are limited to some chakras but without links or continuity with the others, so excluding the rest of the self and the personality – these experiences create a dissociation in the individual, a division in the psyche.

- Experiences of expansion: those that expand the personality, integrating the rest of the factors already existing there but overtaking them harmoniously.

The first ones will originate suffering; the second ones will originate bliss.

The drastic experiences that create dissociation cannot be integrated with the sense of the "I," and there is a lack of connection between thoughts, memories and the sense of one's own identity.

In Yoga, traditionally, pranayama was taught directly from master to disciple; this last practiced under the supervision of the master, probably to avoid problems of dissociation originated by an excess of practice or by a lack of previous preparation. The Siddhas praise the pranayama as one of the more powerful tools for the spiritual growth, but they remark that it could be a double-edged sword if it is wrongly used.

Also, exceptionally, a few people experience spontaneously and intense spiritual experiences (without any previous interest in spirituality) that can create some dissociation; but with time, thanks to a continued practice of Yoga, this practices can be integrated and even used as incentive and reference for their advance. Really, each person is different, with a different past and different strengths and weaknesses.

We must also remark that in Yoga, in reality, we don't look for any experience, but for the cessation of our identification with them. So, we can become aware of the bliss that we already are in essence, regardless of our experiences. In Kriya Yoga we look for this goal even in the turmoil of the world and our daily activities.

The heat of Kundalini

The Sadhana, which is the practice of Kriya Yoga, can be compared to heating water in a saucepan. The heat of the fire, when the water starts to boil, makes the water bubbles from the bottom of the saucepan come up to the surface. In a similar manner, the heat generated from our yoga practice makes different contents appear in our consciousness, like bubbles that surface and explode, and disappear.

It's because of this that Yoga – the real Yoga – is not a practice of insensitivity and isolation from the interior and exterior, but a sharpening of the consciousness that uncovers things that were already there, but had been ignored. There are all kinds of patterns in our psyche, called "samskaras" in yogic parlance, and, like the different layers of an onion, lay between our ordinary state of consciousness and the existence of our Being (which is, according to the Siddhas, absolute being-consciousness-bliss.)

We could compare consciousness with air trapped in bubbles, like small "egos" of consciousness, bubbling and expanding with the heat of the sadhana or spiritual discipline. The air was already there, in the waters of the subconscious, but because of the heat from the spiritual practice it gathers, grows and makes itself visible. Similarly, from the activation of the Kundalini energy from the first chakra, the "egos" of the subconscious start to take root and spread in the consciousness. The appearance of these "blooms" of fragmented consciousness, arising from the psyche of the yogi, take on a life of their own, and can make one most uncomfortable.

Disconcerting as this may be, it provides a great opportunity for growth, because it allows the sadhak to see and integrate the contents of his or her subconscious at a deep level. What can be achieved with sadhana in a very short time would normally take years, perhaps even lifetimes. But, the sadhak must be prepared for this. There are two qualities that are paramount for this work:

on the one hand, devotion – to give oneself unconditionally to Divinity, to the Guru and to one's own growth process ("No matter the effort, my life will serve to gain God"); and on the other hand, detachment – the clarity and the conviction that, come what may, one is not that, but the consciousness that perceives him.

The mind filters

In our psyche there are all kinds of samskaras (conditioned tendencies, impressions and habits) going back to our evolution from the primary animal kingdom. These samskaras, these traits, are not absolute realities but are objects of perception when observed purely and faced squarely. They are like filters that make us see reality in one color, until we realize that we have been looking through a colored filter. Our realization of this tendency can change the way we perceive our world and even this new perception becomes another object, which is ultimately disposable. If we can clearly see the habits and tendencies that have conditioned our thoughts and behaviors, we can cease to identify with their influence. This is the expansion of consciousness that happens when we start to perceive with unconditioned awareness, everything, inside and out. It requires effort (sadhana).

Accept and integrate the contents of the subconscious and just as bubbles burst and the air trapped within them is freed, consciousness trapped and fragmented in the "egos" will be integrated within your own consciousness. Samskaras, impressions, traits and traumas from this life and from past lives make up the content of the subconscious. These samskaras have always been there, influencing your life more or less, directly or indirectly from the front, or hidden in the background, biding their time to surface. Yoga demands, sooner or later, that you process and heal the conflicts in the subconscious to obtain psychic unification and an expansion of consciousness.

Giving full attention to these samskaras – without being

manipulated by them – allows for their assimilation. Unconditional attention or awareness will slowly dissolve them. The expansion of consciousness is only possible when the yogi/yogini confronts and overcomes the control that the "ego," which is normally constrained in a wall of fear, self-limitation and pettiness, has over them.

At the second level initiation we explain, in more detail, different ways of integration of these samskaras, especially those that contain conflicting emotions that can surface after intensive practice.

The Yoga of the Siddhas seeks total transformation. The samskaras, which includes cellular memory, the physical cells small intelligence and emotions, must be transformed. Our mental, emotional and physical bodies are entwined. Such transformation is beyond the human being's capacity alone. The Grace of the Guru, the divinity or the true Self of the individual soul must fully participate. The sadhaka must be willing to relate intimately with the Supreme Intelligence, Light and Power to invoke "superhuman" guidance and support in and through his/her sadhana.

In their ordinary state of consciousness, people are moved by their mental and emotional contents and so follow their own advice, blindly and unconsciously. On the other hand, the yogi, conscious at all times of what is happening on a mental and emotional level is not influenced by it. Realize what is controlling you and take charge; transform what is causes you to suffer and change your life and karma. All that is left is to move toward your "destiny."

The poison that Shiva drank

According to legend, demons and gods agreed to stir the an ocean of milk to obtain the immortality nectar, the amrita. They used the Mandara Mountain as the stirring rod and the snake Vasuki, entwined around it, as the rope. The gods and demons pulled each end of the snake, stirring the ocean. However, the first thing they produced was not nectar but venom, a venom so toxic it could destroy all creation. The gods and demons were frightened, none of them wanted the venom, nor knew what to do with it. Only Shiva, God in the form of a yogi moved by his compassion for humanity was willing to take the venom himself. He took it into his mouth, holding it in his throat without swallowing, turning his throat blue in color. Since that time, Shiva is known as Neelakantha (blue-throated). The stirring of the ocean can be compared with the advanced pranayama practice, in which we make the energy circulate around the spine. However, before we can savor the immortality nectar, we can produce venom.

The advanced pranayama practices can activate the samskaras or patterns lodged in the unconsciousness, some of which are negative; these patterns can emerge in the consciousness. Shiva absorbed these patterns but did not swallow them, meaning that the yogi becomes conscious of these patterns as they emerge, but is not moved by them. He does not swallow them.

The emergence of these patterns should be seen as a unique opportunity to transform them. We seek only the amrita. No one wants the venom, and so we tend to run away from it or project it onto others. Only Shiva, the yogi, accepts the internal venom as an opportunity of transformation. By transforming the venom, one begins to transform egoism and egoistic desires.

Accumulated energy

Our bad habits (anger, desire, gossip, greed, excessive

sexuality, sadness, worry, etc.) are like holes that drain our vital energy, like the water that comes out of a pipe and makes puddles in different sections along our spine. As we work with the chakras, we become conscious of all that energy accumulated around them. Energy can create formations, like scabs covering deep wounds that have not been properly cleansed or have not healed. The formations consists of disturbing mental and emotional habits and impulses developed in this life or from previous lives. As our energy increases due to our intense practice of yoga, these formations around the chakras may also increase unless we cleanse them through such practices as the first meditation Kriya taught in the first initiation seminar. If we do not our bad thoughts and habits become even more evident and annoying. To recognize their manifestation, it is helpful to understand the energy of each chakra and the negative energy formations that may develop around each of them.

Following the chakras order, from the bottom, upwards, this is the type of accumulated material that can arise:

- 1st chakra – Sex and unresolved sexual feelings, not accepted, or integrated.

- 2nd chakra – Fear of life, fear of not having enough.

- 3rd chakra – Pent up anger, repressed from the past and not accepted.

- 4th chakra – Sadness due to abandonment and losses, lack of love.

- 5th chakra – Impulses of denial, self-destructing impulses, repressed self-expression.

- 6th chakra – Seeing "bad" in the world and in the environment.

- 7th chakra – Not being present, evasion, estrangement from God.

To cleanse and transform these energies it is necessary:

First, to discover the mental and emotional habits that create them, those are like holes that drain the energy: fears and ordinary worries, anger and being upset by trivial things, stress, etc.

- Then we need to see, accept and transform the "karmic residues" or the samskaras or patterns that remain there:

In the process of transformation it is very convenient to remember that energy is not destroyed, but transformed; repression is not the solution, transformation is. Very common formations are accumulations of repressed sexuality and anger, because as children we are taught that "being good" implies not experiencing those things. The integration of both elements requires us to first accept the energy patterns because they exist, but then to find another outlet for them, so they can be transformed. Sexual energy, for example, is a very powerful tool that the yogi utilizes to open the upper chakras.

In an ideal state all chakras are activated and realize their function to serve the yogi's awareness, concentration and emotional balance, without losing energy. Some affirmations for each one of them, like thoughts that express their ideal functioning, would be:

- 1st chakra – I accept, use and transform the sexual energy into spiritual energy.

- 2nd chakra – I thank God as the only source of all provision and security.

- 3rd chakra – The energy comes from God; all my acts are offerings to the Divinity.

- 4th chakra – I think and live from the heart; I flow in love's flow; To love and serve others is to love and serve God.

- 5th chakra – I accept silencing the ego and follow the creative voice of God / the internal Guru/ my Supreme Being.

- 6th chakra – The Divinity is behind everything that I perceive, as creator and maker.

- 7th chakra – The Divinity is present with me here and now.

The commotion of samadhi

When a yogi has done years of intense practice he can experience an expanded state of awareness, beyond the ordinary state of consciousness. Such expansion is called "Samadhi" in Yoga and, reading the classic "Yoga Sutras" of the Siddha Patanjali, one can see that there are many types of Samadhi or "cognitive absorption." The experience of the Samadhi or the expansion of consciousness takes one far beyond the normal boundaries of the mind.

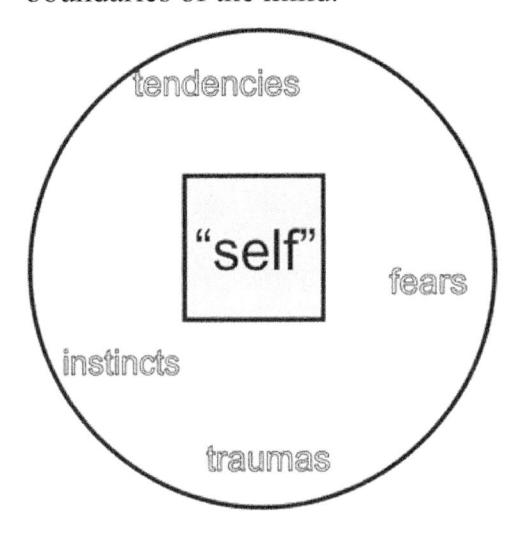

Some times on the spiritual path we talk about "dark nights," and these happen often after the first transcendental experiences. The excellent book "After the Ecstasy, the Laundry," by Jack Kornfield, narrates many of these "dark nights" experienced by spiritual aspirants. There is a Zen Koan, which asks: Why, after experiencing the state of ecstasy, the monk falls in the well?

I will try to explain the reason for that "dark night" with the graphic shown in the next page.

Our habitual state of consciousness would be the square within the circle, our little "ego," or "what we think we are," is a small area, with padded walls of our beliefs, ideologies (including spiritual ones), likes and dislikes. Our likes give us emotional compensation for all that we are constantly trying to avoid. These preferences and aversions create the walls that hold and strengthen the ego self.

The heightened experience of the Samadhi is like a strike of lightning that offers us a split-second glimpse into and experience of the totality of who we are. The totality is represented by the circle, which covers all of the existence, beyond the claustrophobic precinct beloved by our little "ego." This experience happens normally during meditation, after years of intense practice.

It is a joyful experience, according to the Siddhas because joy is the true nature of the Being. It is an experience of expansion, which begs us to answer the questions, "How do I return to the small precinct demands of my ego? The being is no longer satisfied with the limitations imposed by those four walls.

So we leave behind what was our home, our reference territory, before samadhi, but since we have not yet managed to cover the totality's territory, the Being that we are, we find our self dissatisfied. What was good enough before no longer satisfies us. The spiritual apprentice is now in "no man's land," with no way of turning back, it seems.

And what does he see before him? A vast deserted land, which has some things that he did not think existed, but that are between him and his vision of the horizon: past traumas, fears, instincts, negative tendencies; everything that Jung the psychologist called "the shadow," amplified and totally visible. Everything that he had forgotten a long time ago (or even a few lives ago), come back with force. Faced with this, the first reaction is, to flee. One is experiencing the "dark night."

Yamas and *niyamas*

Purification is necessary all along the way. But there are times when periods of intense cleaning are necessary. This is one of them. Sometimes the life and mind of the yogi can be liken to the legend of Hercules, who was ordered to clean the filthy stables of King Augias, which had never been cleaned. It was a demeaning job and almost impossible to do, even for a semi-god like him. We must understand that really, we do not only cleanse our psyche, but also part of the collective subconscious. All kind of things are bound to spring up that oppose spiritual advancement and it all must be integrated and transmuted.

The yogi, logically, cannot continue to live unconsciously. He must review all his life habits, for he cannot continue to feed all that had so blatantly hindered his expansion of consciousness.

The Siddha Patanjali, in his Yoga Sutras, cites the eight famous aspects necessary for the spiritual experience. The first two, and the base of the whole process, is the practice of certain restraints and disciplines, the *yamas* and the *niyamas*. It is at this time that we come to understand why we need them in order to advance spiritually.

The yamas, or restrictions, are non-violence, truthfulness, non-stealing, sexual restraint and greedlessness.

The niyamas or observances are purification, contentment, austerity, self-study and devotion to the Lord.

Apart from following the yamas and the niyamas, it is imperative to review our own mental and emotional habits, and integrate all karmic residues that resurface to the consciousness. Nobody has said that Yoga was easy. This process is the real transformation, something that traditionally, in India, was carried out under the stern discipline of a Guru. Even Yogananda, an exceptional being mentions how he "was purified in the daily flame of the punishment" under the stern discipline of his Guru. The traditional guru-disciple system in India has not been exported to the Western world, perhaps not only because it is rare to find true realized gurus willing to work on disciple's egos, but also because it is even rarer to find true disciples willing to submit to that kind of discipline. But, in its own way, our life will work to discipline us if we walk the spiritual path and choose to take advantage of karmic lessons to work on our own limitations.

From that moment on, spiritual advancement can be likened to the colonization of new territories, the discovery of new wild lands, all the while, integrating them into daily life. Samadhi widens the light of consciousness, taking in all the shadows, without judgment or regard to where they arose, individual or collective (perhaps both). Yoga is a process of expansion; it is not a process of restriction or contraction: consciousness embraces everything, leaving nothing outside it, while remaining totally unattached to it all. The yogi continues his Yoga until he finds himself free and experiencing Yoga with an unlimited consciousness.

Bhakti Yoga: the bliss of love

Of the five powerful limbs of Babaji's Kriya Yoga, none of them is more potent than Bhakti Yoga, the Yoga of love and devotion. As we understand now, consciousness is the path and the goal of our practice; through consciousness we understand the real Self, the permanent in an impermanent world. Consciousness helps us to understand the Self. But there is another piece to solving the game of consciousness and that is the cultivation of love, which helps us understand the why of creation itself. It seems, perhaps that the existence of the world can only be understood from the point of view of love. In the path of the Siddhas, Shiva (consciousness) loves and honors Shakti (the energy, that is, the creation), and Shakti loves and worships Shiva. The infinite and the finite intermingling in an endless dance.

Consciousness and love become the two wings we need to reach Self-realization. Yoga could be defined as the practice of quieting the mind and opening the heart, a formula that brings the experience of bliss. In our normal state we do just the opposite, unless we change our tendencies: our mind is overheated and our heart is cold and closed.

Buddhism equates the development of consciousness with the development of compassion; Jesus himself talks about bread and wine – about sharing the consciousness (bread) and the bliss and love (wine) of the master.

The fivefold path of Kriya Yoga recommends the cultivation of love in a systematic way as another yogic practice: Kriya Bhakti Yoga. We cannot force love, it comes out naturally from inside of us, but we can cultivate it daily by creating a space where it can manifest.

It is said that love is one of the qualities of our true self that flows naturally and without effort in the state of realization. But, as we are not self-realized yet, we can cultivate this flow through different practices: devotional chanting, selfless service to others, practice "feeling" the presence of the Divine, and regularly seeing the divine form in everyone.

The French are great lovers of cheese; they have more than 600 varieties of cheese. The Indians are great lovers of the Divine, they have a full variety of possible relationships between the individual and the Divine, which can be considered as father, mother, friend, beloved, etc. God, the Absolute has a thousand names, each one of them emphasizing a different aspect. The different gods are different personifications of the one and only Self, the essential reality. The practitioner of Bhakti Yoga chooses an aspect of the Divine to attune with and channel his/her love and devotion and aspiration toward. There is great power in the spirit of devotion, even if it is as a scientist who is devoted to truth. The Self can be loved in its impersonal aspect, as the Truth of existence. There is a sublimeness in devotion to the Divine in everyone; the power of one is multiplied, multiplying the objects of inner bliss, getting closer to the universal vision of oneness.

Babaji's Kriya Yoga is not a religion, sect or cult; it is a technology to improve all aspects of life. It is for anyone. Anyone can benefit from these techniques, regardless of his creed or religion. Bhakti Yoga techniques encourage students to cultivate a loving, devotional, compassionate nature, in his own way.

The practices of Kriya Yoga raise subtle energy in the subtle spine to the top of the head, the crown chakra, where our potential for realization of the absolute consciousness lies. It is impossible for energy to reach the crown chakra and abide there without first penetrating the heart. The more open the heart, the more the energy will rise. And the happier we will be.

Yogic techniques are a necessary part for our spiritual growth, but acquiring the balance necessary to stay in the higher chakras comes from the cultivation of love and compassion. The mutual and equal expansion of consciousness and love will create the breakthrough we seek. Realized masters, by example have shown that the follow-up to Realization is unyielding compassion and unconditional service. The One who has mastered Yoga loves his fellow man as himself. When the "I" disappears, who can be called the other? The joys and pains of the other are his own.

Love, the universal vision of the One, closes the circle of creation, where the One, who became many, becomes again one, in the middle of the endless delight of diversity.

Appendix: Beginning Babaji's Kriya Yoga

Start to experience Babaji's Kriya Yoga with the practice of the 18 asanas of Kriya Hatha Yoga. These 18 asanas are the only kriyas of the 144 kriyas that can be learned outside the initiation seminars, you can learn them in the booklet "Babaji's Kriya Hatha Yoga: 18 postures of relaxation" or in the DVD "Babaji's Kriya Hatha Yoga: Self-Realization through action with awareness." And continue with "Babaji's Kriya Yoga: Deepening Your Practice." These can be ordered through this website:

http://www.babajiskriyayoga.net.

If you feel attracted to Babaji, you can tune into His inspiration and His grace through the chant or repetition of His mantra "Om Kriya Babaji Nama Aum." Babaji tells us, "take one step towards me and I will take ten steps towards you."

The rest of the techniques of Kriya Yoga are taught in three initiations:

- First initiation: together with the 18 asanas of Kriya Hatha Yoga, the student learns Kriya Kundalini Pranayam – the most important technique in Kriya Yoga, which, among other benefits, will greatly accelerate your spiritual evolution. Yogi Ramaiah said that one year of practice of this technique equals 11,864 years of spiritual evolution. The student learns also 7 meditation techniques, to gradually master the mind.

The 23 techniques of the First Initiation are the basis of this path of Kriya Yoga; the student never stops practicing them, even when he learns more advanced techniques.

What can I expect after the first initiation?

Do not go looking for dramatic "spiritual experiences," in the practice of Kriya Yoga. Instead, expect your practice to increase a sense of calm, happiness, mental clarity, better concentration, insight, inspiration and discernment in your life. These are the qualities of the higher self, your real Self. The goal of Kriya Yoga is to manifest these qualities more and more in daily life.

Some students are satisfied with just these practices in their lives, noticing the benefits obtained. Others want to deepen in the experience of Kriya Yoga, they want to receive mantras and more understanding about how Yoga works so and they attend the advanced Training Initiations:

- <u>Second initiation</u>: a weekend retreat where one learns how to integrate the practice of Kriya Yoga in the daily life: while eating, working, sleeping... The retreat culminates with a consecrated fire (Mantra Yagna) and the initiation in the mantras of Kriya Yoga.

After a year of practice of the techniques of the First Initiation, the student can attend the Third Initiation:

- <u>Third initiation</u>: a training of one week, where all the 144 kriyas are learned or reviewed. These are a set of rich and diverse techniques, which help to bring an integral development in all the levels of the being: physical, vital, mental, intellectual and spiritual. It includes also the kriyas learned in the first and second initiations. Two Mantra Yagnas are celebrated, and the students receive more mantras, finally learning the "samadhi" techniques, the state of breathless communion with the Self or Absolute.

If you want more information you can check the website www.babajiskriyayoga.net. My website (in Spanish) is www.kriyayogadebabaji.net.

Glossary

Ananda: divine bliss. The bliss of Self, which does not depend upon external circumstances.

Ashram: residence of a yogi.

Chakras: literally, "wheels." Subtle psycho-energetic centres which are distributed in the human body.

Dharma: the principle of righteousness, of what is correct and appropriate, which is inherent to all creation, sustaining it.

Guru: literally, "who dissipates darkness." Spiritual teacher and guide; one who teaches how overcome the *gunas* the modes of nature.

Japa: mental repetition of God's name.

Karma: the consequences of action, words and thoughts, which can be negative or positive, bringing suffering or happiness to oneself and others.

Koshas: five sheaths that uncover the Self: physical, emotional or vital, mental, intellectual and spiritual.

Kriya: literally "action with awareness." Yogic technique.

Kundalini: our potential power and consciousness that can be awakened through the practices of Yoga.

Kundalini Yoga: Yoga that seeks to awaken the Kundalini energy (located under the base of the spine) and to bring it up to the crown chakra, in a sublimated form through various practices.

Mantras: sacred syllables or divine sounds, given by realized yogis, which generates a higher energy and consciousness on those who repeat them.

Mantra Yoga: Yoga based in the constant repetition of the names of God.

Nadis: subtle channels of energy or prana.

Prana: vital energy.

Pranayama: Yoga techniques that use breathing to achieve different effects at a physical, emotional and mental level.

Sadhana: spiritual practice or discipline.

Samadhi: cognitive absorption; mental silence breathless state of union with the Absolute.

Samskaras: habits stored in the subconscious mind.

Satguru: supreme guru.

Shakti: energy, Divinity's feminine principle or the energy which shapes the entire universe.

Shaktipat: energy transmission from teacher to disciple.

Shiva: the Lord; the Absolute; Divinity's masculine principle or pure consciousness.

Siddha: literally, "to be perfect." Wise men that developed the scientific art of Yoga.

Vasanas: tendencies stored in the subconscious mind.

Yamas: the restraints, as formulated in Patanjali's Yoga Sutras: do not harm, do not steal, be true, be chaste and do not be greedy.

Yoga: India's ancient philosophy, psychology and practice, aiming to achieve a healthy and harmonious existence and Self-realization. According to Sri Aurobindo, a great modern yogi, "Yoga is a generic name for any discipline whereby the individual tries to overcome his ordinary mental consciousness, in order to achieve a greater spiritual consciousness."

Bibliography

- (1995). *Yoga Vasishtha*. Madrid: Etnos.

- Aurobindo, Sri. (2003). *The integral Yoga*. Twin Lakes, USA: Lotus Press.

- Govindan, M. (2004). *Babaji and the 18 Siddha Kriya Yoga Tradition*. St. Etienne de Bolton, Quebec: Babaji's Kriya Yoga and Publications.

- Tirumular Siddhar. (2010). *The Tirumandiram*. St. Etienne de Bolton, Québec: Babaji's Kriya Yoga and Publications.

- V. Zvelebil, Kamil.(1993). *The poets of the Powers*. California: Integral Publishing.

Other books in English by Nacho Albalat, Nityananda:

Yogic teachings of Jesus
The experience of the Kingdom of God

Nobody in the West is as famous and as unknown as Jesus, despite our culture being built around His teachings. "Yogic teachings of Jesus" compares the mystical teachings of Jesus with essential texts from the yogic tradition of the Siddhas from India. Raised in a strict Catholic culture, the author felt the need of integrating the figure and teachings of Jesus with his practice of Yoga. So he wrote this book to reconcile both views, for himself and for others in a similar situation.

The wisdom of the Siddhas, the masters of Yoga, allows us to reencounter Jesus' direct and radical message, a message that still moves us, even after two thousand years. Through "Yogic teachings of Jesus," the reader can meet the Beloved teacher, and rediscover the freshness of His words, the "living waters" of Truth, beyond limited interpretations. It is also a great introduction to Yoga for Christian people.

This book proposes a trip that, travelling through Orient, ends in our own heart, the place in where, according to the Master, the Kingdom of Heaven lives.

Advancing in Yoga
The path of Kundalini, the chakras and the Siddhas

"Advancing in Yoga" offers clear, useful and practical guidance on how to develop Kundalini, your potential power and consciousness and the chakras, the psychic energetic centers in your vital body.

"Yoga" refers to union with the Self and the disciplines which result in it. The Yoga of the Siddhas deals with the awakening of kundalini and the chakras, and in so doing, expands your consciousness beyond the limits of ordinary human nature. Old habits and tendencies resist change. This book is an essential aid for the advancement and transformation process of the committed Yoga student.

Topics include development of the "Heart Witness," sadhana (yogic discipline), the bliss of the Self, freedom from negative tendencies, aspiration, Grace, each of the chakras, the perfection realized by the Siddhas even in the physical body, advice to initiates regarding the advanced kriyas.

It also includes instructions to accompany the Babaji's Kriya Yoga practice, and offers alternative techniques for Yoga students in general.

Printed in Great Britain
by Amazon